Steps Toward Abundant Living

Steps Toward Abundant Living

◆

A Christian Perspective

Carey N. Ingram

iUniverse, Inc.
New York Lincoln Shanghai

Steps Toward Abundant Living
A Christian Perspective

iUniverse books may be ordered through booksellers or by contacting:

iUniverse
2021 Pine Lake Road, Suite 100
Lincoln, NE 68512
www.iuniverse.com
1-800-Authors (1-800-288-4677)

Because of the dynamic nature of the Internet, any Web addresses or links contained in this book may have changed since publication and may no longer be valid.

The views expressed in this work are solely those of the author and do not necessarily reflect the views of the publisher, and the publisher hereby disclaims any responsibility for them.

ISBN: 978-0-595-47059-4 (pbk)
ISBN: 978-0-595-70777-5 (cloth)
ISBN: 978-0-595-91341-1 (ebk)

Printed in the United States of America

Contents

Acknowledgments

First and foremost, I must say thank you to my Heavenly Father. He has allowed me to undertake the writing of a second book. It is my purpose here to share my thoughts and inspire people that "we can do all things through Christ who strengthens us." (Philippians 4:13)

I am always indebted to my darling wife, Judy, who encourages and inspires me to write; I must write. I hope that my writing does make a difference. To my children and grandchildren who are my pride and joy: I hope that one day when You, Christian (5 years old), and Christa (2 years old) can read, perhaps these words will encourage and inspire you. Much of this writing is with BOTH OF YOU in mind.

Mrs. Laney Stevenson, I want to thank you for your help in editing my book. Your academic ability and our shared colloquialism give me confidence that this book will be easy to read and to understand.

Ms. Charlene Ransby did the book cover idea and illustration. She has served me and the Lovejoy Baptist Church as secretary and administrative specialist with untiring vigor. Thank you, Charlene, for your patience and caring.

I want to add Brian Smith of Tech PC to my list of thanks. When my laptop crashed, Brian, painstakingly, went beyond what he should have to ensure none of my work was lost. Several chapters of my final draft would have been lost had it not been for Brian.

As always, I send greetings and a shout out to my beloved Lovejoy Baptist Church Family. They serve as a home base for all my ministries. With their support and encouragement, I am challenged to do more to serve this present age.

A very special thanks to Ms. Lisa and Doug Jones for their consultant services, to Mr. Thomas Moore for his advice and editorial support, and to Mr. Robert Finnell, who when I was discouraged, encouraged me to move forward. Thanks for being there for me, Mr. Finnell.

Some great ideas and messages expressed in this book are not mine. I want to thank Mrs. Charlotte Thomas, Rev. Robert E. Houston, Sr. and Dr. A. L. Patterson for giving me permission to share their work with you.

Finally, I thank my Grandmother, Leila Marie Maddox, who went to be with the Lord before this book was completed. However, it is because of her life, those fond memories of her, and our long talks together all of which compelled me to complete my writings on this subject. She is my hero and I dedicate this book to her.

Foreword

"I have ridden the shoulders of my mother
and my father to arrive at my today.
"I hold their hands as I test the strength of my legs
to climb into my tomorrow."
(taken from an African rite-of-passage ceremony)

Growing up in the 1940's with parents just coming out of the Great Depression of the 1930's was, according to our parents, a not-so-easy life. For those who were already struggling, the Great Depression simply added to the hardships of trying to provide the bare necessities of one's family.

Our parents were, among other things, mill-hands working for less than minimum wage but certainly resourceful in that they always managed to make ends meet. We remember the "rationing" lines for many food items, but our parents dealt with these situations and provided well for their families. We do not recall ever being hungry or cold.

We both had loving, caring parents who loved their families and above all, who loved their God. Worshipping God and having Him at the center of their lives was paramount in our homes. "Remembering the Sabbath Day to keep it Holy" was not an option in our homes. No one asked us if we wanted to attend Sunday School or Church. It was understood that we attend regularly. No questions asked. "Am I My Brother's Keeper?" reigned not only in words but in deed in our neighborhood.

Thank God, we were both introduced to a loving God, by way of parents, at a very early age. We both united with the Baptist faith during our pre-teen years. It goes, without saying, that change is inevitable. Life, itself, is full of changes and challenges-some good and some not so good, but God was and still is that *Constant* in our lives.

Down through the years—elementary and high school, Trade School, a Military Duty, College, Finding Life's Work, Marriage, Becoming Parents, and eventually Retirement and then becoming more involved in our community in an effort to give back, the one thing that has been *Constant* in our lives is our *God.* When we lost our son, one of the most trying times in our lives, it was and still is our God who continues to be a Sustainer, A Rock, and our Eternal Hope. Friends have marveled at how we have managed to deal with this great loss and yet have continued to move forward with our lives. Very simply put, it is our God—*Our Constant* in the midst of Life's many challenges. We have learned to lean heavily on Paul's words to the Church of Rome: "And we know that all things work together for good to them that love God, to them who are called according to his purpose." (Romans 8:28)

"Living an abundant life" is a personal journey we each must set for our own religious aspirations with Divine Guidance. For us, Abundant Living involves making God the Center of our lives, accepting His Will in our lives and serving our Fellowman. It is giving back a portion of what God has given us. Having a profound love for youth, we have attempted to demonstrate this love through our involvement with several Outreach Ministries in our community.

Having served as a minister and pastor for some 30 years, Pastor Ingram has done more than simply proclaim the Gospel. He has exhibited the true meaning of "living an abundant life" by his love for his God and his Fellowman. His generous volunteerism has earned for him many awards, among which are Minister of the Year and Heart of The Community Award. As his grandmother before him blazed a path of serving others as God has ordained all of us to do, Pastor Ingram continues this Tradition and lives an exemplary life as evident in his unselfishness in serving others. His life is a testimony to the following scriptures:

"FOR I WAS AN HUNGRED, AND YE GAVE ME MEAT:
I WAS THIRSTY, AND YE GAVE ME DRINK: I WAS A STRANGER AND YE TOOK ME IN: NAKED, AND YE CLOTHED ME: I WAS SICK, AND YE VISITED ME: I WAS IN PRISON, AND YE CAME TO ME. THEN SHALL THE RIGHTEOUS ANSWER HIM SAYING, LORD, WHEN SAW WE THEE AN HUNGERED, AND FED THEE? OR THIRSTY, AND GAVE THEE DRINK? WHEN SAW WE THEE A STRANGER, AND TOOK THEE IN? OR NAKED, AND CLOTHED THEE? OR WHEN SAW WE THEE SICK OR IN PRISON, AND CAME UNTO THEE? AND THE KING SHALL ANSWER AND SAY UNTO THEM, VERILY I SAY UNTO YOU, INASMUCH AS YE HAVE DONE IT UNTO ONE OF THE LEAST OF THESE MY BRETHREN, YE HAVE DONE IT UNTO ME." (Matthew 25:35-40)

When asked by Pastor Ingram to write the Foreword to this book, *Steps Toward Abundant Living*, we felt so very humble and even unworthy. Thank you, Pastor Ingram, for such an Honor as we know there are so many more individuals who are more deserving of this honor than we. Most important, we thank you

for not only sharing with us in words a Christian Perspective for "living an abundant life", but also for being a role model for all of us who are attempting each
day to be worthy to experience God's many blessings.

John N. and Laney Montgomery Stevenson

Laney M. Stevenson is a retired teacher from Rome City Schools having taught
high school English for 31 years. Upon retirement, she taught at Coosa Valley
Technical College for 15 years in its GED Program. She is a community volun-
teer serving area Youth in After-School Programs and in a Rites-of-Passage Program for elementary school-aged girls.

John N. Stevenson is retired from General Electric Company after 31 years. He
has been a Deacon in the Baptist Church for 44 years. He is founder and Coordi-
nator or Godfather Ministry of Rome, Inc. A businessman, he owns his own Jan-
itorial Service.

Both John and Laney are active members of the Lovejoy Baptist Church. In
1995, both John and Laney were named "Child Advocates of the Year" by the
Rome/Floyd County Commission on Children and Youth. They are recipients of
numerous community awards including Heart of the Community Award—John
in 2001 and Laney in 1998.

High school sweethearts, John and Laney have been married 47 years. They have
an adult daughter, Lanetta, and a granddaughter, Briana. An adult son, Stanley,
is deceased.

Introduction

Stop

It was immediately following the tragedy of 911 that I came to realize that I did not feel as secure about life (my life and life in general) as I once had. As time passed, I came to see that my queasy nervous stomach, irritable behavior, and feelings of doubt about myself were something more than what had happened on September 11, 2001. Have you, like me, ever had what I call a "dark cloud" feeling hanging over you and there is no explanation for it? You may call it mid-life crisis, a rite-of-passage to old age, or maybe just an attempt to understand yourself better. It was then that I decided to write down my feelings and perceptions as to what was happening to me and how I could deal with those feelings and perceptions so that at the end of the day I could feel good about myself and the world around me. One thing I am convinced of: We owe it to ourselves to make life a happy experience. What has been reinforced to me is that each individual with God's help can make that happen.

Steps Toward Abundant Living is my sharing of those Biblical Principles and common sense factors that when applied to circumstances and situations in our lives (whether good or bad) can result in a greater adventure (abundant life). I call these Biblical Principles and common sense factors *Steps,* but they are not in any sequential order merely representations of the phases of life that we must pass through successfully with the help of our Almighty God. I have simply dedicated my life to these trains of thought and have learned to apply them when they are needed. This book is about the application. Determine that you can and will build upon the life God gave you and that life will flow in abundance.

There is a passage of scripture in the Bible on which I built the message of this book. They are the words of our Lord and Savior Jesus Christ: "The thief cometh not, but for to steal, and to kill, and to destroy: I am come that they might have life, and that they might have it more abundantly. I am the good shepherd: the good shepherd giveth his life for the sheep." (John 10:10-11)

At the beginning of this passage, Jesus defines Himself as the door by which all men shall come through to be saved. All that have come before Him were robbers and thieves. They did not come to give to man, but rather to take life away from him. In order to relate to his followers, Jesus declared Himself to be the Good Shepherd, and those who come into the pasture by Him are His sheep. Jesus, the

Good Shepherd, loves us so much that He was willing to give up His life for us. In fact, His only purpose for coming into this world is to ensure our having a blessed life, and having an abundance of God's love.

At the age of seven, I opened my heart to God and walked through "the door" and received my salvation. At that time, I did not understand all of what it meant to be saved. I did not fully understand the abundance of life that was given to me through Jesus Christ. However, I did notice a change in my thinking and my attitude. I knew that I was indeed a new creature and even at the age of seven I felt a calling on my life. Slowly but surely, I began to realize that I was special and that I sensed a purpose and a direction for my life.

Truly, I can say that I have been blessed all of my life. The odds of my even being alive or going to college were slim; but thank God, I am here and have achieved a Master's level in Higher Education with military and seminary training as well. I married my childhood sweetheart and we have been happily married now for 32 years. We have walked through life together and the Lord has blessed us with three beautiful children. We now have grandchildren who make us feel even more blessed.

If I had the opportunity to change my life or to be someone else completely, I would not change a thing. I have certainly had my ups and downs, my trials and tribulations. Temptations have come and sometimes I have fallen flat on my face, but, nevertheless, I thank God for all that I have gone through. I realize now that all these things have made me who I am now. I thank God that I know who I am, why I am here, and where I am going. It is my observation that many people go through life never knowing these basic things about themselves. This book is about finding a way towards that abundant living. I pray that this book serves to help and inspire others to know that they, too, are special and that God, through Jesus Christ, has definite plans for your life. No matter how old you are, where you are, and regardless of your circumstances, the best is yet to come.

It has taken me 50 plus years to fully realize my worth and my blessings. In fact, a series of difficult circumstances has served to bring the best out of me. That being said, I envision going even farther in my pursuit of an abundant life. It is not about fame and fortune or power and prestige. These things have their place, but greater than these are the simple but genuine relationships with those around us. Abundant living is about making use of the time we have. It is about being liberated, about being who you are and feeling good about it at the same time. It is giving and asking for nothing in return because there is nothing received that can bless you more than what is given. It is about loving those who love you as well as those who don't because abundant living is about loving the least of them. It is growing from being a babe in Christ to being a mature Christian, a disciple of Christ that allows you to mentor others so that the legacy of the good and abundant life continues long after you have gone to be with the Lord. I am in the midst of this growth and I want to share how I have come to this place in my life that others might experience life as God intended.

Finally, abundant living is about the choices we make. God has made us free agents. We can choose to go through the door of the Good Shepherd and live, or we can choose to simply exist and never find and fulfill our destiny. I am convinced that the following words I am about to share with you will help you find and fulfill your destiny. My baby girl, Michelle, shared a short essay with me that sums up my introduction as we step toward abundant living.

Choice of Consequences

Each moment of my life is defined by a choice. With each decision comes a negative or positive outcome and though lies can sometime blind my perception of the person I am, the deception never changes the person I am destined to become.

With each of my choices there comes a higher level of maturity and a wisdom that dwells within, waiting to shine as an external example of peace and humility that truly defines who I aspire to become. With each choice, the mystery of me begins to unfold. I am learning to be my own person and to trust in myself.

I have also learned that in the choices I make I never have compromised my ideals or lessened my passion to live up to my full potential. Because I know that my choices not only affect me, but also can affect others who potentially follow my example.

Consequently, I choose to love me, respect who I aspire to be, appreciate the person God blesses me to become and, ultimately, I choose to be me. I realize that the greatest choice I have ever made was accepting Jesus Christ as my Lord and Savior. Yes, it is all about choices. Be careful of your choices because with every choice comes a consequence.

Dedicated to the memory of

Leila Marie Maddox
(May 20, 1913–October 18, 2003)

Step I:
How It All Started

It was Wednesday, September 12, 2001 and Randy Davenport, Jeff Allen, Jim Smith and I were driving on I-20 East. At exit 278 we turned off and headed to New Birth Missionary Baptist Church, led by the internationally known Bishop Eddie Long. We were on our way to worship with him and the New Birth Congregation in Atlanta while attending a Pastor's Enhancement Skills workshop at the ICAM Institute at the Interdenominational Theological Seminary. We were all seeking some help, healing, and encouragement. It had been a great workshop so far, but we didn't need schooling that night; we needed to worship and fellowship. For this was the Wednesday after THAT TUESDAY, 9-11, the day of the Terrorist attack on New York's Twin Towers and the Pentagon in Washington.

Like everyone else, we were devastated by what we had witnessed on television the day before. I can still remember watching Katie Couric on the Today Show that fateful morning as she was coming back on the air from a commercial break, and began to inform her audience that something had occurred at one of the Twin Towers. The camera switched to the scene and it appeared that one of the towers was on fire. At the moment I saw this, it never entered my mind that it was something other than a serious fire and that firemen would come and put it out in a reasonable short period of time. As I watched the events unfold, I was rushing out the door to catch the bus that had arrived at the Renaissance Hotel to take us to our class on the ITC Campus. When we got to the campus, I went straight for the television in the lounge area. I arrived just in time to see a plane disappear into the other tower. Then the explosion, a burst of flames in the building and I knew this was more than just a fire caused by some electrical malfunction. I knew that something serious was happening right before my eyes. In less than twenty minutes, the report came that a plane had exploded into the Pentagon in Washington, D.C. It was terrifying. It made my stomach churn. Within a short period, I felt what we all felt: vulnerable, fragile, and frightened. I could not help but think, are we at war, where will this kind of destruction take place next? I thought about my wife in Rome, my children scattered across the south at various college campuses. I wanted to be near them. I wanted all of us to be home together.

That morning at about 10:30, we finally assembled ourselves together in the classroom. Our instructor, Rev. Dr. Franklyn Richardson, Pastor of Grace Baptist Church in Mt. Vernon, New York had been late because he was watching the television in his hotel room with great concern. Some of the congregants of Grace Baptist Church were employees in the Twin Tower Buildings. Were they there for work this morning? Were they safe? Could he fly home? All these questions concerned Rev. Richardson. He had talked to his wife and determined that first and foremost what he could do at this time was to go to class and minister to those of us who were at this seminar.

It must have been God's favor that had me in Atlanta at that workshop, and not at home involved in my routine schedule. I say that because if I had not been at the seminar, I would not have heard the great message of hope that Rev. Richardson delivered. There were only about 15 of us in attendance but I think the whole world would have benefited at hearing what was said in his 10-minute devotion. He read Psalms 46 and told us what it meant to him, and while he was speaking, I was able to make notes and by the following Sunday, I was able to give the congregation at Lovejoy Baptist Church the hope of God that had been given me. Here is an excerpt of the morning message at Lovejoy, September 16, 2001:

What do you do when the worst that can happen happens? What do you do when the earth shakes and fire lights up the sky and everybody you turn to has the same look of fear and uncertainty that you have? What do you do when you feel so vulnerable and fragile, when in an instance we are forced to deal with our own mortality? What do you do when it seems that your whole world is spinning out of control and there is nothing you can do about it? I think it is safe to say that all of us have experienced some emotions like that this week.

When things in your life seem unsteady, you must find that which is stable and hold on to it. There has been a lot of hugging and holding recently because it gives us some sense of strength. I stopped by to tell you today that I know nothing more stable than the solid rock, Jesus. He is the "rock of ages" and as the hymn goes, "Rock of ages cleft for me, let me hide myself in thee." Another song goes, "Jesus is a rock in a weary land, a shelter in the time of a storm." Our scripture today is also a song of hope and comfort. It is a solemn tune that was sung by alamoth or the women who sang the soprano voice in the temple choir. The point is the scripture was to be sung by the best singer. Psalms 46 is a special praise, a song of Holy Confidence and is as follows:

"To the chief Musician for the sons of Korah, A Song upon Alamoth. God is our refuge and strength, a present help in trouble. Therefore will not we fear, though the earth be removed, and though the mountains be carried into the midst of the sea; Though the waters thereof roar and be troubled, though the mountains shake with the swelling thereof. Selah. There is a river, the streams whereof shall make glad the city of God, the holy place of the tabernacles of the most High. God is in the midst of her; she shall not be moved: God shall help her, and that right early. The heathen raged, the kingdoms were moved: he uttered his voice, the earth melted. The LORD of hosts is with us; the God of Jacob is our refuge ... Be still, and know that I am God: I will be exalted among the heathen, I will be exalted in the earth. The LORD of hosts is with us; the God of Jacob is our refuge. Selah." (Psalm 46:1-7, 10-11)

I think you will agree with me when I tell you that this scripture speaks to us. But let me give you the heartbreaking news about our plight this morning. God's presence and power operate in our lives and in our country to the extent that we need Him: (1) We must belong to Christ, and (2) We must not only be a hearer of the word but a doer of the word as well. As the trouble of a dying world unfolds before us, people have been praying and seeking the Lord like never before in recent history. But what are we seeking Him for? Generally speaking, we are seeking solace, comfort, and an easing of the pain and sorrow. We want Him to make us feel safe again and to assure us that everything is going to be all right. But I'm afraid that too many of our prayers fall on deaf ears, not because God doesn't care, but because we don't really care until we get in trouble. Now that the world looks like it is coming to an end, we feel like God ought to step in and fix things for us. But God sees bombings, destruction of property, devastations, poverty, wars, and violence (all as a result of sin) everyday throughout the world. Now that we Americans see destruction so up close and personal we seek the Lord and want His immediate attention.

The truth is God wants to give us the attention we need, but He is not a puppet on a string. You can't pick Him up when you need Him and then when everything calms down and you feel safe, go back to business as usual without Him. No, when God has our full attention, what we need to do is to repent of our sins and give our life to Him because He is showing us repeatedly that He is our only hope. When I saw with my own eyes the tragedy and terror of the attacks, I was devastated. I could not believe that it was really happening. I was very concerned about how you were doing, and naturally how my family was. But thank God, in just a few hours, the Lord brought to mind my prayers that morning before all this had happened. Then I thought in terms of the promises of God. He promised in His word never to leave me. He further promised to be my shield, my protector, and my refuge. I, then, began to claim all of that and God began to put me at ease. Why? He put me at ease because I am His child, and as His child, I have His assurance that He will watch over me and my family. Yes, Tuesday was a glimpse of the end of time, but the fire we saw in the sky was a fire that came from man, up from the earth. The fire we must concern ourselves with is the fire that God rains down from above. And just like Tuesday, when that day comes, there will be nothing we can do. Our hope is to be ready.

As Christians, we should not be too alarmed by terrorist attacks, school shootings, or presidential assassinations. They are the signs of the times. We just need to be ready when Jesus comes. Listen, I don't make light of anything that has happened this week as all of it was tragic and terrible. Life as we know it has changed forever. I don't feel nearly as safe today as I did last Sunday and I know that we will never fly the same, or have the same desire for tall buildings again. The real tragedy of Tuesday is that not only did thousands of people lose theirs lives, but also some of them lost their lives and souls. Of all the news reporting, no one will say how many perished and went to heaven, but the Heavenly Herald had a report that said something like: Brother Ben Faithful died in a plane explosion, absent from the body, present with the Lord. Sister Borna Gan died in the Twin Tower fire, absent from the body present with the Lord. And you see, beloved, in the final analysis, that is the only thing that matters: where you go when you leave here because everybody is going to leave here. We don't know when and we don't know where, but we know that we all must die. No problem. The problem is being ready so you can go be with your maker when you die, and to do that you must be Born Again. So I rest from my first point which is in order for God to be your refuge, You Must Be Born Again.

Now, my second point that assures the believer of God's refuge is we must not only be hearers of the word, but doers of the word as well. We must practice what we preach. I often think of my beloved country, America, one nation under God. On our currency it says, "In God We Trust", yet formal prayer in school is against the law and the government has little to do with prayer in its daily business. We are a society that requires by law that church and state be separated. So we hear the Word, but do we really do the Word as we proclaim in America? A scripture comes to mind when I think about America today in light of our crisis:

"He, (America) that being often reproved hardeneth his neck, shall suddenly be destroyed, and that without remedy." (Proverbs 29:1)And we can apply that to our own individual lives. That's why I want us to be careful as a church family that we always do right by our people. Because everything we've got, God can snatch from us in the blink of an eye. Inhale, you got everything, exhale, and it's all gone. Isn't that what happened the other day?

So what am I saying? Very simply, I'm saying we made a covenant with God that is not only to be looked at, but also to live by. And God will keep His word, and will take care of us and meet our needs when we walk in His light. Proverbs 3:6 says, "In all thy ways acknowledge him and he will direct our path." So when trouble comes, we can truly depend on Jesus. We can have a talk with Him, and He will talk back to us, ease our pain, and help our grieving hearts. He will forgive us of all our sins, but we must earnestly ask Him. Do you feel sick? He's the great physician. Do you feel weak? He'll be strength. Do you feel naked? He will clothe you. Does your soul thirst? Jesus will quench your thirst. Do you seem to always be in a financial bind? Trust Christ and watch Him share His wealth with you. We've got to take off our righteousness, and put on His righteousness. There is nothing too hard for Him. He loves us so much. We simply must belong to Him. We have to be sincere and we can't fake it. We must love Him with all our heart, and if we do that, there isn't anything He won't do for us. There is nothing Christ dislikes more than for His people to make a show-thing of Him, and not use Him. He loves to be employed by us. The more burdens we put on His shoulders, the more precious will He be to us. One thing I know: He loves us; He cares for us.

The German Theologian Martin Luther said of this Psalm: "We sing this Psalm to the praise of God, because God is with us; he powerfully and miraculously preserves and defends his church and his word against all fanatical spirits, against the gates of hell, against the implacable hatred of the devil, and against all the assaults of the world, the flesh and sin."

So what do you do when the worst things that can happen, happen? What do you do when you don't know what to do? Well the Psalmist says, "Be still." The songwriter said, "Be Still, God will fight your battle; be still, God will fight your battle; be still, God will fight your battle; God will fight your battle if you just keep still." Then, remember who God is and experience Him. Remember, this is His world, and He's got the whole world in His hand, and you as well. He has never lost a battle, and He's never lost a case. He's got Healing hands. He can destroy; yet, He can defend. Most of all, remember He is still on the throne. So you can put your hands down. There are no emergencies in Heaven. Nothing frightens our God and nothing alarms our Father. Put your hands down; your Father is watching over us. We think we have to do something but know that God is your Father and when the ground stops shaking, he says, "I'm still God." God is unchanging and His promises are still true. . What he said in the sunshine is true in the rain.

After the seminar given by Rev. Franklyn, Rev. Davenport had gotten in touch with Bishop Long about worshipping with him and later one of the New Birth staff members had contacted us and given us directions. He had even made preparations for us to stay for dinner. I cannot begin to explain to you how beautiful and sprawling New Birth Missionary Baptist Church facilities are. I would simply suggest that if you are ever in the Atlanta area, let this church be a place to visit and to worship.

I was driving our church van. Lovejoy Baptist Church, Rev. Carey N. Ingram was written on the side of the van and they recognized us as we entered the entrance gate. There we met our armor bearer for the entire evening, a young man who was with us from start to finish. We were privileged to ride right up to a special parking section for all of Bishop Long's guests. We had been friends since our early days in the ministry though I had not seen him since then. He was pastor at Cedar Springs First Baptist in Cedartown while I was a few miles away in Rockmart, Georgia as pastor of Zion Hill First Baptist. Since we were so close, we exchanged revivals and other fellowships on a yearly basis and were good friends. But God moved us in completely different directions both in location and styles of worship. Rev. Eddie Long became Bishop Eddie Long, pastor of one of the world's largest churches in America, and I remained Rev. Carey Ingram of Lovejoy Baptist Church, pastor of one of the world's smallest great churches in America. I remained more traditional in worship and Eddie became more innovative and progressive. Needless to say, we were looking forward to seeing each other.

As we walked around New Birth Baptist, I felt like a country bumpkin gone to the city. I stood in awe of everything around me until we actually walked inside the 7,000 seats auditorium. One thing about me is when I go into my Father's house, I let go and let God. As a traditional Baptist preacher, we don't practice a lot of things that full Gospel Baptist Churches do. But this has never mattered to me. I believe in praising God; I believe in making a joyful noise, and I believe that worship should be lively. Why I have come close to being put out of Pentecostal churches because of my own special brand of fervor. Once we entered that auditorium I heard one of my favorite praise songs, "Never Seen The Righteous

Forsaken," and I simply surrendered to the Spirit. I danced right up to my seat. It was the beginning of a wonderful, uplifting fellowship, one that we all needed. I enjoyed myself in the Lord and it was also a blessing to see so many people so unified and turned on to God. I don't know if this was regular worship or if it was due to the tragedy the day before, but the spirit of the Lord was upon all of us in that place. We wanted Him; we needed Him and He was there and did not disappoint us.

Bishop Long did a masterful job of reminding us that God is still in charge of this world, and though it would take time, God would heal all our hurts from what we had just experienced. One of Bishop Long's gifts is that he is the best at making you think he's talking just to you. His eye contact with his audiences is truly a gift of God. I shall be indebted to him and Rev. Richardson for helping me through the 9-11 Crisis. Without them, I might not have been able to effectively minister to my loved ones back in my home and with my church families.

Throughout the service as I sat, or stood and rejoiced, I began to sense from God that I needed to address the issue of how we must live daily in the face of adversity. It was obvious to me then more than ever that we live in a world of uncertainties. I am not one who promotes the doomsday spirit, but I think you will agree with me that these are difficult and perilous times. We live in a world full of unfriendly and mean people who have no regard for life or for what is sacred. There are also things happening all around us that we have no control over, yet they tremendously affect our lives. The sayings are like clichés but they are true; we have money, but no wealth; medicine, but no health. We have recreational places and leisure time, yet we do not know how to relax. As Americans, we live in the free world, yet we are caged by being the most medicated and drugged up people in the world. We are the most blessed, yet the most stressed.

I was thinking about the events of yesterday as well as the challenges of everyday life, and I knew I wanted to do something and say something to give people hope. For as devastated and helpless as I was and, yes, depressed for a while, two things never left me: my hope and my joy. I never doubted that God would get me through this period. I also knew that we, as people of faith, would rally together and help others to get past the crisis, hurt, and pain. But as God always does, he would take a negative and turn it into a positive. For me that meant writing about how we can cope with life when life seems more than we can bear.

We all desire to live our lives as if we were standing on top of the world. But, what do we do when we feel as if the world is standing on top of us? Well, I share this information with you because I know that there are several things that I have learned to do over the years that help me to keep my head above water even when it seems the world around me is drowning. I want to encourage you to know that there are some steps you can take that will indeed allow you to live abundantly in spite of the world around you.

Step II:
Grandma—An Unfeigned Faith

On October 11, 2003, I was privileged to be the keynote speaker at the Thankful Baptist Church in honor of Pastor and Mrs. Nim Russell. It was an uplifting worship and fellowship. A highlight for me came when Minister Brandon Crowley, one of my associate ministers at Lovejoy, introduced me. In his remarks, he talked about how <u>Ebony, Forbes, Sports Illustrated,</u> and other magazines annually listed the most influential people in their fields. These were people, he said, who oftentimes become our heroes because of the great things they do in society. However, he went on to say that our real heroes are not the ones we read about; rather, they are those people who have literally touched our lives—those everyday folk who inspire us and influence us on a daily basis by the simple things they do. We notice their faith, their courage, and determination in their very simple walk of life. They rarely make the newspaper, win national accolades or travel the world. Real heroes are those who have changed our diapers, wiped our nose, walked us to school, and taught us in Sunday school. Moreover, without any fanfare, they have lived exemplary lives before us. They have encouraged us to the point that we not only want to be like them, but also to become confident in ourselves. Then, this remarkable young man concluded by saying that I had been one of his heroes. As I walked to the podium to speak, I thought to myself, "This is why you live a godly life so that others might be encouraged to do likewise."

One week later, almost to the hour of that wonderful introduction, I received a telephone call to come to the Sunbridge Nursing Home to say good-bye for the last time to my hero, my Grandmother, Mrs. Leila Marie Maddox. Jesus declared: "I am come that they might have life, and that they might have it more abundantly." (St. John 10: b) Of all the people who have lived such a life, my grandma (as we called her) was one of them. It is from her life that I had come to understand just what it means to live life abundantly. It is not all good or bad, rich or poor, and neither is it always in your favor. You do not always gain the desired results of what you strive for, but your losses are never beyond what you can recover, and the trial always makes you a better person. The abundant life is a life with Christ that almost immediately becomes an adventure. It is exciting and challenging with never a dull moment. Even at rest, you can quietly and meditatively plan your next move. What I saw my grandma do that yielded such a dynamic life is best shown by our Lord in another verse of scripture: "Give, and it shall be given unto you; good measure, pressed down, and shaken together, and running over, shall men give into your bosom. For with the same measure that ye mete withal it shall be measured to you again." (Luke 6:38)

My grandma was a giving person in the truest sense of the word. I marvel at how she loved people and always had something to give even to the least of them.

She was born Leila Marie Walker in Newnan, Georgia, May 20, 1913. She was the only child born to Beaulah and Felix Walker. Beaulah died before Marie was one year old and so after her mother's death she moved to Temple, Georgia where her Aunt Dilsy and Uncle Steve Walker reared her.

Marie moved to Rome in 1930 where she lived the rest of her life. It was the time of the Depression era in America. Yet, against those odds, my grandmother forged ahead to do some very special things in the next 50 years. She married and gave birth to two darling baby girls: Mabel and Mary. Mary, the baby girl, would grow up to have two sons: Kenneth and, you guessed it, me. My mother and grandma were free spirits. That is to say, they were very independent women (at least in thought). They were not afraid to try anything. I lived with my mother when she lived in Rome, but my mother would often leave town for a better job. By my choice, I would always choose to stay with my grandparents. No one ever had a problem with that so I really had the best of both worlds.

In 1934, my grandma joined the Springfield Baptist Church and became a devout Christian lady. My grandfather worked at the local gas company and purchased a large 5 bedroom house with a basement right next door to the church. My grandmother with only a seventh grade education, was as resourceful as they come. In her lifetime, she had several careers as a presser at a local dry cleaners and as a licensed hairdresser (as they were called in those days). She owned and operated a beauty shop and fruit stand at Five Points in Rome for years. As she grew old, she moved her business to the basement of her home. When some of her clients grew older and could not come to her shop, she would go to their homes and oftentimes perform her duties for free. I know because I went with her most of the time. She used to call me her "shadow." Not only would I, as a child and even in my early adolescence, "cry" to go with her on her jobs, but I always wanted to follow her to church. She was, without a doubt, the inspiration that led me to seek the Lord, which ultimately led me to answer the call of the ministry and preach the Gospel.

My grandma (often against my grandfather's objections) shared our home with strangers. If someone came to town and she realized that they had no place to stay, she would simply invite them into our home. They would stay there until, in her words, "They got on their feet." Some of these people would oftentimes be sick, or have addiction problems. None of that mattered. She would assist them in finding help for their sickness, and oftentimes lead them to Christ while helping to deliver them from their addictions. Sometimes they would pay her for staying with us and sometimes they would not. Other times if a construction company brought men into town to work on building projects, she would always rent out a couple of our rooms to them. Really, it was a boarding house because not only would they live with us, but she would also prepare breakfast in the morning and supper for these men in the evening when they came from work. Now, this was definitely for profit and was, at times, quite lucrative. It was always fun for the family. We would get to know these people as if they were part of our family. We shared stories and watched TV in the living room. It was really an education for me. I learned how to get along with people who had different ideas from what I had been accustomed. Sometimes the influence was bad, but most of the time it was good. My grandma always pointed them to the church that was right next door. She did not insist, but it was hard to refuse a woman who had cooked, made your bed, and shown you kind hospitality.

I also remember how some of our neighbors didn't like the idea of strangers staying in our neighborhood. Their cars and work trucks would be up and down the street we lived on. A good many of these men, who sometimes brought their wives and small children, were homebodies. They brought their guitars and played them loudly on the front porch. Some enjoyed the nightlife and would come home late at night waking the dogs and the neighbors. None of this ever seemed to bother my grandma. She just went right on minding her business. If there was ever any kind of disorderly conduct, my grandma would handle it, and my grandfather would always come to the scene to back her up. "Straighten up or get out" were the only words of discipline at our house. We rarely had any problems with people staying at our house.

I remember several men who stayed at our house were sickly and some were terminally ill. Through my grandma's love and steadfast witnessing to them, they accepted Christ as their Savior, and sometimes a short period later, they would die. Being so close to life and death and seeing my grandma make such a difference in people's lives so near to death and possibly eternal damnation made a profound impact on my life. I would see them make a change, a real change and leave this world with the hope of Christ. She often told her family, "I always wanted a house by the side of the road so I could be a friend to mankind." I do not know where she came across this but I know that her theology and philosophy is summed up in a poem that she often recited in her life:

"The House by the Side of the Road"

There are hermit souls that live withdrawn
In the place of their self-content
There are souls like stars, that dwell apart,
In a fellowless firmament;
There are pioneer souls that blaze their paths
Where highways never ran-
But let me live by the side of the road
And be a friend to man.

Let me live in a house by the side of the road,
Where the race of men go by-
The men who are good and the men who are bad,
As good and as bad as I.
I would not sit in the scorner's seat,
Or hurl the cynic's ban
Let me live in a house by the side of the road
And be a friend to man.

I see from my house by the side of the road,
by the side of the highway of life,
the men who press with the ardor of hope,
the men who are faint with the strife.
But I turn not away from their smiles nor their tears,
Both parts of an infinite plan-
Let me live in a house by the side of the road
And be a friend to man.

I know there are brook-gladdened meadows ahead
and mountains of wearisome height;
that the road passes on through the long afternoon

and stretches away to the night.
Still I rejoice when the travelers rejoice,
and weep with the strangers that moan,
nor live in my house by the side of the road
like a man who dwells alone.

Let me live in the house by the side of the road
Where the race of men go by.
They are good, they are bad, they are weak; they are strong,
Wise, foolish-so am I.
Then why should I sit in the scorner's seat,
`Or hurl the cynic's ban?
Let me live in my house by the side of the road
And be a friend to man.
—Samuel Walter Foss—

My grandma practiced Christianity. She was one of those kinds of people who was there when the church doors opened. Whether it was Sunday school, Church Worship, Bible Study, Revivals (at her church and all over town), Missionary Society meetings, or Church Teas, my grandma loved the church. She was not just a member, but also a leader. For years as President of the Missionary Society she would organize monthly food deliveries for the sick and shut-ins. She was careful to see that people had food to eat especially toward the end of the month when their funds were low. She was a substitute Bible School and Sunday school teacher and she organized our Youth Department and made sure we always went on a Sunday school picnic.

She organized our church's first Vacation Bible School and was the head of the Church's Kitchen committee for years. She attended local Associational meetings as well as the State and National Conventions from which she would come back with fresh ideas and would persuade Pastors and Deacons to try her plans. Nothing seemed to give her joy and strength like going to church.

I told you how I cried to go with her to these functions. Well, in her latter years when she was barely able to get about, guess who wanted to follow me as I began doing ministry and revivals? You guessed it—my dear grandma. And just as she was patient with me, turn about was only fair play. I really enjoyed her company many nights coming back from church, discussing the Lord and what had taken place at church that night.

She worked until she was about 70 years old. She drove a car until she was about 75. After a series of small wrecks (like knocking over mailboxes and running into other cars), my brother literally took her car keys and refused to give them back to her. Even at this time of her life, she sold Avon Products and was a nurse's aid in private homes helping those who were physically less fortunate than she was. When she stopped work completely, she still volunteered at the local Girls Club. She could knit and crochet sweaters and other things like that.

Once as Mother's Day was approaching, I sat at my desk prayerfully, wondering and meditating on how I would address this special day in a sermon. I was led to Paul's word to Timothy:

> "When I call to remembrance the unfeigned faith that is in thee, which dwelt first in thy grandmother Lois, and thy mother Eunice; and I am persuaded that in thee also. Wherefore I put thee in remembrance that thou stir up the gift of God, which is in thee by the putting on of my hands." (II Timothy 1:5-6)

The key words that stuck out in those verses were "unfeigned faith." In laymen's terms, unfeigned faith is not being a hypocrite, but rather being genuine and sincere in what you believe and do. My grandma demonstrated her faith in God by the works she did. Believe it or not, she was often criticized and ridiculed by some who just did not understand, but it never seemed to bother her. I know that the people that she did these kind deeds for loved her dearly. She was affectionately called Marie by friends of her age, and called Ms. Marie by those who observed her and by those she helped. Many of my friends called her "grandma" just like me. She was not perfect; yet, if you knew her, you knew what she stood for; that Faith and works do go together. We must believe that God is who He says He is and that He can do what He says He can do and that He desires to use us to perform the godly tasks of life. My grandma exemplified faith and works.

One gets the impression from Paul that Lois and Eunice, the mother and grandmother of Timothy, must have faced tremendous odds rearing and training Timothy in a Christian atmosphere. We know that there was no man present in the home. We know that the Christian church was in its genesis state at this time and faced much opposition. Yet, these ladies remained steadfast in their belief and the results produced a fine young Christian minister that Paul regarded as his "son in the ministry". What a compliment to the efforts of these two ladies.

Unfeigned Faith is what every child of God needs. From Paul's use of the word, unfeigned, I get the impression that sometimes we can allow our circumstances and situations to cause our faith to become shallow. Perhaps, when we need faith most, we become less sincere about it because of the consequences. The biblical definition of faith is found in Hebrews 11:1: "Now faith is the substance of things hoped for, the evidence of things not seen." For me, faith, then, is a certain amount of uncertainty. We do not know what the end will be, but we have to patiently wait on God to bring that which we hope for. This kind of uncertainty can be like a weight on us, physically and emotionally. These times are when we must draw upon the spirit of God by saturating ourselves in prayer and in the word of God. I know for myself that faith in God means trusting solely in God through His word regardless of what things appear to be.

Remember this acronym for faith: F—forsaking, A—all, I—I, T—trust, H—Him—Forsaking All I Trust Him. I suggest that in a Capitalistic Society with computer analysis, economic challenges, social and psychological advisors, and governmental management, it is easy to see why faith in God is oftentimes put on the back burner of life. Society does not tell us to wait patiently on God, but rather it tells us to get all you can as soon as you can. Do it unto others, before they do it unto you. This is the world's way. It is a selfish way, and in many instances, it yields a false sense of security of life.

Matthew 16:26-27 says, "For what shall it profit a man, if he shall gain the whole world and lose his soul? Or what shall a man give in exchange for his soul?" What good are your possessions if you are terminally ill? What comfort is there in the American way if you do not know where your teenage child is at 2 a.m. in the morning? In times of war and terrorism, how do you relieve the stress of uncertainty? After all is said and done, where will you spend eternity? We must remember that there is more to life than the life we live here on this earth. There is a hell to shun and a heaven to gain.

What is our resolve? Unfeigned Faith!!! Yes, I suggest that there is a lesson to be learned from Lois, Eunice and Marie. As Christians (especially Christian leaders), we must "build our hopes on things eternal and hold to God's unchanging hand" for our own sense of being and stability. Moreover, we must do this for those around us. In due seasons there will be people placed in our lives who will need to know that there is something greater than power, prestige, and position. Certainly, all these things shall pass away. We must be the privileged few who tell others that there is One who is from everlasting to everlasting, but the only way to have access to Him is by faith. It is one thing to tell people of our faith, but it is a greater service when people see it working in our lives.

My grandma's life and example challenged me. She challenged me by the things she said and by the things she did. She also challenged me by the things she did not do because when the going was tough, she did not give in. She held on to her faith. Her example taught me not to succumb to the trappings of this world. "Do not allow yourself to become desperate, wavering, or frightened of the uncertainties around you", she often said. "Remember, you have an advocate who always goes before you, a doctor who has never lost a patient. He is not practicing medicine. He is medicine. You have a lawyer who never lost a case. You have a judge who is just, righteous, and more than fair. He looks beyond our faults and sees our needs. You have a friend who has already gone through what you are dealing with now. He has promised to stick closer to you than a brother. All God asks of us is to walk by faith and not by sight. Trust Him and lean not to your own understanding. Have an unfeigned faith and know that godly results will follow." I hope by now that you can see the parallel between Lois, Eunice and Marie. These were ladies of faith. They were not preachers, but they produced preachers. They did not go to college, write books, or do anything that would cause them to make the cover of a national magazine, but they lived life in such an abundant way, in such a Christian way, until it affected those around them tremendously.

My grandma had such a positive impact on my life. In the last five or six years of her life, she was legally blind and, at times, confined to her bed. She lived with us in our home until her condition was such that she had to be institutionalized. Even then, I would sit and talk with her and gain so much wisdom. I could ask her anything and she would always point me to Christ. "Hold on; keep the faith Carey; this, too, shall pass" was one of her constant refrains to me. Oftentimes, I would go to her and share time with her and know instinctively what her answer would be, but I simply wanted to hear her say those special words that she could say that would lift my spirit. She did not leave our family any money for all she possessed when she left this world was that old wood framed five bedroom house next to the church where she had labored all of her life. Just a few months before here death, she strongly suggested that my brother and I donate that house to the church and we did. During the last days of her life, she was blind, sick and very feeble, but she was still giving. She was still that lady of unfeigned faith. She was my hero.

On October 18, 2003, my grandma quietly moved from time to eternity. "Absent from the body, we are present with the Lord." (2 Corinthians 5:6) I know that she is resting peacefully until the appearing of our Lord and Savior, Jesus Christ. Though she had lived 90 years, it was hard for me to let her go, but I did. I had some difficult days afterwards, but time has helped me to adjust to not having her around physically. Otherwise, I talk to her and talk about her almost every day. In fact, my wife and I are constantly laughing and talking about what grandma would say, think, or do if she were around to help us with whatever it is we might be going through during the course of a day or week. You know, when you lose someone you love dearly, you can always find strength and solace in those fond memories. You do not have to say "Good-bye." You can say, "I'll see you later."

A young lady, Ms. Charlotte Thomas, who is a virtuous woman in our life today, was also influenced by my grandma and wrote this poem that now hangs on my wall in my study at home:

"Fond Memories of Mrs. Marie"

God's Missionary she lived to be, serving others continuously.
Teaching, studying and sharing His Word
To those who listened as if they had never heard …
It's all about the love of Jesus she wanted us to know.
If we would just trust, believe, and obey
To Heaven we, too, can go.
Her soft-spoken voice made it so plain.
We have nothing to lose but everything to gain!
So why can't we take this missionary's advice
To follow—accept our only real sacrifice
Remember He Arose—He's not dead!
And she'll arise too—Ain't that what He said?
She'll meet Him in the air and said we can too …
Because it is about God's Mission,
so what are you supposed to do?

It's not too late to accept God's will
If you'll just get busy—Don't sit still.
You'll fulfill Life's Purpose as never before
You'll know why you're here and … God's Blessing will pour!

Mrs. Marie, truly a living witness for all to see,
just look at Kenneth and Ca-rey!
Her love for God sustained them and their families—
Now they all know that they, too, can lean on God's love and

promises—through Christ Jesus—they have been redeemed!
And it's all because of Mrs. Marie, The living Missionary
they witnessed Early ...

Step III:
The Power of Prayer

"Call unto me, and I will answer thee, and shew thee great and mighty things, which thou knowest not." (Jeremiah 33:3)

In my almost 50 years of life, if I could pinpoint the one thing that has literally changed my life for the better and forever, it would be my discovery of the power of prayer. For me and for those who do it consistently and fervently, we can witness that it transcends your life. It is, without a doubt, one of the most valuable tools that Christians have to impact not only our lives, but those around us. Further, I have come to believe that God will, at times, call upon those of us who I call "prayer warriors" to pray for specific situations to ward off calamities.

When I was 13 or 14 years old, I was told the following story: It was the year 1958. At four years of age, I developed an intestinal disorder. My mother and grandma took me to the doctors, Dr. Matheny and Dr. Black. The pediatricians literally held my life in their hands because for whatever was wrong with me, they determined that I needed surgery. The worst-case scenario was if something was not done, I could lose my life. My doctors hoped that surgery would correct the problem and ease my pains. It turned out that my intestines, for some reason, were tied in knots such that I could not have a bowel movement. It was something beyond constipation because I could not relieve myself in any way, and I was oftentimes vomiting.

After the surgery, I showed signs of improvement. The pain was gone and I seemed to be able to go to the bathroom just like anyone else, but my folk's hopes were soon dashed. Within two weeks, I was back in the hospital in pain with the same diagnosis that I previously had. That meant a second operation only weeks apart from the first-all at the tender age of four. This time they had to remove a small portion of my intestines from certain areas and connect them again. My grandma recalls the evening they brought me back into the hospital room after this critical surgery: She said, "The doctor brought you in the room and declared that they had done all they knew to do. They said you were stable, but had a high fever. They did not give you much hope for survival, but I told the doctor to just give you to me. I held you in my arms and began to pray. I told the Lord what you meant to me, and if it would not be asking too much to spare your life that you might grow up to be something special for Him one day." Afterwards, she got on the phone, called all her prayer partners, and told them to please keep me in their prayers. Day by day, I got better. In fact, the only evidence that I had ever been so sick was the scars of my operation incision that covered my entire lower body. One scar is clearly visible on my body even to this day. I used to be so embarrassed by that scar, especially as a teenager in the locker room, but now I see it as the evidence of the fight for my life. Satan wanted to take me out, but because of good doctors and the prayers of the righteous, I not only survived but 48 years later, I'm able to write and tell you all about it. You can believe me when I tell you there is power in prayer.

My definition of prayer is communication (that is to say conversation) between man and God. Man reaches up to God and God reaches down to man. Prayer requires having the proper attitude, which means before you verbally talk to God, your mind and body must be in a humble state of being. After all, you are about to talk to the Most High God. To me that means getting somewhere in solitude, positioning yourself in a worship position (kneeling, head bowed, prostrate on your face, and mentally withdrawn from the world). It takes time to converse with God, and then to meditate so that He might speak to your inner being. I repeat. It takes humility and time to really commune with God. Imperfection cries out to perfection; the soul of humanity interacts with the divine tribunal and says, "I love you, I need you, help me." That takes humility and it takes time. In the process comes an intimacy between you and God that I cannot fully explain. You will have to experience that for yourself. It brings about a bonding, an inner peace that allows you to move forward through your day with confidence and with the assurance that you are not alone. The very Hand of God guides you with a stern, but gentle touch.

Prayer should always be an expression of thanksgiving and a confession of sin and guilt with a request for forgiveness. Prayer can also be an intercession on behalf of others such as your family, friends, leaders of the church and community, circumstances and situations, the sick, and your enemies. Anytime, anywhere, for a reason or for no specific reason, the Bible declares, "Men ought to always pray." (St. Luke 18:1)

Prayer is a personal contact with your maker. Can you imagine that God loves us so much that He gives us prayer as a means of always being able to contact Him? The Bible is full of men and women at prayer, some standing with hands lifted up to God, others kneeling, and still others falling before an altar. Some mumble and mourn inaudibly while others cry aloud. Some pray spontaneously while others are liturgical and repetitious. People pray in the synagogues, at the temple, and at churches, but prayers can also be heard on the street, in your home, and in your closet. I want to suggest to you where I believe the most powerful place there is to pray, and that is to say, where the greatest results are realized is in that personal private secret place. Hear the scriptures:

> "Take heed that ye do not your alms before men, to be seen of them: otherwise ye have no reward of your Father which is in heaven. Therefore when thou doest Thine alms, do not sound a trumpet before thee, as the hypocrites do in the synagogues and in the streets, that they may have glory of men. Verily I say unto you, they have their reward. But when thou doest alms, let not thy left hand know what thy right hand doeth: That Thine alms may be in secret: and thy Father which seeth in secret himself shall reward thee openly. And when thou prayest, thou shalt not be as the hypocrites are: for they love to pray standing in the synagogues and in the corners of the streets, that they may be seen of men. Verily I say unto you, they have their reward. But thou, when thou prayest, enter into thy closet, and when thou hast shut thy door, pray to thy Father which is in secret; and thy Father which seeth in secret shall reward thee openly. (Matthew 6:1-6)

I attended the annual E.K. Bailey Pastor's Seminar held in Dallas, Texas a few years ago. One of the facilitators was Dr. Warren Wiersbee, an elderly Bible Scholar, author, Pastor, and Pulpit Humorist. He is internationally known, having done a complete commentary on the Old and New Testament. At the end of one of his sessions, one minister asked him a question: "Dr. Wiersbee, how have you come to be the man you are in respect to your work and dedication to preaching and proclaiming God's Word with such simplicity and clarity?" Dr. Wiersbee's answer was, "I spend time with God in prayer." He talked about how he wakes up early in the morning before everyone else when it is quiet and gets on his knees. Then, he has quiet time with God. He shocked us all when he said this might easily take 45 minutes to an hour just opening his heart to God in the quiet and stillness of the morning. Afterwards, he gets up and prepares for his day which includes time for prayer and devotion with his wife. Once he gets to his office, everyone on his staff knows that the first hour or so is more time alone for prayer, Bible Study, and meditation. Obviously, only after these hours are spent in prayer, Bible study, and meditation is he ready to take on the responsibility that awaits him that day. This routine is done on a daily basis.

When I heard this great testimony, I was, to some extent, ashamed of my prayer life. I have always been a person who prays, but I must confess it was not ever for any long period of time, and certainly not with the intensity that I know it requires now. I know God has always heard my prayers and I have always been able to see the results of my prayers; however, I have come to realize that prayer to God that will yield greater results, feed the soul, and prepare one for the great work of the cross in this troubled world requires our complete attention. Needless to say, my prayer life has never been the same after hearing Dr. Wiersbee's simple discourse on his routine. He told us of his early Morning Prayer time. He did not get into how he prayed throughout the day and into the evening, but as a Pastor, I know that prayer is really an ongoing process. The Apostle Paul tells us in 1 Thessalonians 5:17 to "Pray without ceasing." We should never allow Satan to cause us to think that we are not worthy to call on God in prayer—that is to say, we should never allow our problems, something bad we did or said, or any circumstance overwhelm us to the point that we feel we can not go to God in prayer. The scriptures declare: "Let us therefore come boldly unto the throne of grace, that we may obtain mercy, and find grace to help in time of need." (Hebrews 4:16)

There is an old adage that many of you are familiar with that demonstrates the idea of the power of prayer in our lives and it goes like this: NO PRAYER … NO POWER, LITTLE PRAYER…. LITTLE POWER, MUCH PRAYER … MUCH POWER. I declare unto you when a person spends quality and quantity time in secret prayer with God, he will respond and life takes on a completely new meaning.

The words that God spoke to Jeremiah in Jeremiah 33:3 sums up the power of prayer in our lives: It was the 10th year of King Zedekiah, the last years of Israel, God's chosen nation as a United Kingdom. All that King David and Solomon had built was now being conquered and destroyed. At this time, God was using his prophet, his preacher, Jeremiah, to warn his people of the impending dangers and absolute captivity by the Babylonians. God called for Israel to repent and then and only then could they return to their homeland. Jeremiah gave God's word, and demonstrated his faith in this prediction by using his personal savings to purchase a field in Judah. Now these were difficult times for Jeremiah. The leaders of Israel (particularly the military leaders) did not want to hear the word surrender. Jeremiah had been around for years, and they were tired of his messages. He had been in and out of prisons and dungeons because he dared to tell God's people what God was saying instead of what they wanted to hear. These were times of trauma.

Around the city of Jerusalem, they could see the Babylonian camp fires and hear the cries of war slowly but surely approaching. The homeland was in chaos, gripped by internal wickedness, crushed by the external enemy. Jeremiah told them not to fight at this time, but just surrender and in time God would rescue his people and return Israel to a former state. This kind of talk fell on deaf ears. It caused low morale among Israel's soldiers, and landed the prophet Jeremiah back in prison. There in prison Jeremiah began grumbling and complaining. It was at this time that God came to Jeremiah for a second time and spoke three distinct particles of truth: (1) "Call unto me, (2) and I will answer thee, (3) and shew thee great and mighty things which thou knowest not."

Prayer is commanded, he said. "Call Unto Me." We are not merely counseled or recommended to pray, but rather bidden to pray. What a privilege it is to be able to go before God's Throne of Grace. We miss blessing upon blessing when we do not pray. It is like having soup kitchens well stocked in the winter season. Those who are poor and hungry may receive food by going to the door and asking. Yet, there is nothing in the constitution or federal laws that force people to go and get this nourishment. My grandmother used to say, "You can take a mule to the trough, but you can't make him drink."

Now, if prayer is so powerful and yields such wonderful results, why is it that our prayer life is oftentimes so shallow? Well, simply put, it is a trap of Satan that keeps us from praying. Satan sends us what I call, "Fits of Worldliness." He knows how to keep us occupied with the things of this world. He keeps us busy and occupied with doing "natural things." We never forget to eat, to sleep, to go to work, to go to the rest room, or to lock our doors at night. We are so caught up in the natural things—things that come easy and things that give immediate gratification. Beyond that, Satan keeps us tired—so tired and too tired. You go to work and come home—so tired. You go to the table so tired and hungry until you do not bother to give thanks for the food you are about to eat. Then you get in your easy chair (if you happen not to be going out that night for a ball game, etc.) and watch hours of TV. You are so tired you often fall to sleep in your easy chair. Again, you are too tired to pray. So, you get into bed and go to sleep.

Someone said sleeping is the most dangerous time of you life because you are not conscious, not aware of your surrounding and completely helpless to the world around you. Yet, we are too tired to ask God to watch over us while we sleep at night. We are so tired in the morning after a night of sleep that we lie there until the last possible moment for us to get up and go to work on time. Now we have to rush to get to work because that job is so important. Satan is behind all of this. He keeps us too busy, too tired, too sleepy, and too late to pray. Does it strike you as strange that we give our freshness and vigor to the natural things of life, and give our slothfulness to the things of the spirit? We spend hours at ball games, watching TV, reading the newspaper and magazines. Yet, when it comes to Bible reading and prayer, we are just too busy and too tired. Well, if you do not have time to keep your life in good spiritual shape, then you are indeed too busy. Satan does all he can do to keep you from your power base—your power source-Prayer.

God commands us to "Call Unto Me" throughout the Bible. He says to, "Call upon me in the day of trouble, and I will deliver thee." (Psalms 50:15) "Seek ye the Lord while he may be found; call ye upon him while he is near." (Isaiah 55:6) "Ask, and it shall be given, seek, and ye shall find, knock and it shall be opened unto you." (Matthew 7:7) "Watch and pray, lest ye enter into temptation." (Mark 14:38) "Continue in prayer." (Colossians 4:2) These are just a few quotes from the Bible where we are commanded to pray.

Now, the obvious question is how can I break this terrible, natural cycle that causes me to neglect so great a source of power and strength for my life? The way that I broke that cycle was to do some rescheduling. I literally went to my appointment book and started scheduling prayer and devotional time. My wife gave me the idea years ago when she would get my appointment book and block days, mornings, or afternoon that she set aside for "family time." I learned to do the same thing for my personal time with the Lord. Guess what? It works. It has worked so well that now my natural schedule includes plenty of personal time with the Lord. Let me give you just a few examples of what I am talking about. First, each time the Lord allows me to see another morning, I get up going down on my knees. By now, my body and mind are so conditioned that I can get up early enough to spend as much time as I need to pray in the morning before I leave my house. How long is that? Well, I have learned to pray in the morning until I am satisfied that God is satisfied.

Sometimes, when I wake up in the middle of the night to go to the rest room, or if I just cannot go back to sleep, that is prayer time—yes, even getting down on my knees. I have also discovered that God does not mind one bit if I read a devotional book while I'm sitting in the rest room. My schedule also consists of never leaving my wonderful wife and home until we pray together. When I get into my car to go over the highways of life, I have found that is an excellent opportunity to ask for travel grace just before I turn the radio on. Before I leave my driveway in the morning, I have already prayed three or four times. I've made it a practice to never eat until I pray for the rich bounty with which the Lord has blessed me. What about the evening hours of leisure? If the TV is worth two hours of my time watching a movie, is not our God worth at least the same? When you talk to someone on the telephone, have you ever thought about making it a point to pray before you end the conversation? This will cut out a lot of phone time and leave even more time for devotional and prayer time. People do not call as often when they know the end of the conversation means praying over that which you just talked about. The good part about this is you will soon begin to enjoy this time. You actually look forward to waking up and praying in the middle of the night. It becomes something very special and precious between you and God. You feel more refreshed in the morning and your attitude changes toward everything and everybody. You are on your way to living an abundant life.

Now, I will examine the second particle of truth, "I will answer thee." We should not tolerate for one minute the ghastly and grievous thought that God will not answer prayer. There is nothing too hard for God who shows loving kindness to thousands and who has majesty, dominion, and power. He is great in counsel, mighty in work; God is full of grace and truth, slow to anger, quick to mercy. He is the great and awesome God who would not even withhold his only begotten Son, but instead sent Him to be a ransom to ensure a way for us and to give us a chance to live in fellowship with Him forever. Can we suppose the God of heaven, whose nature is love, could tear one of his own from his bosom of mercy? No matter what troubles we get ourselves into, no matter how we act toward the Master … He Cares. Even when we were guilty and sinners, not fit to live, and not ready to die … God cared. He will come to our rescue and answer our prayers as we are his very own. He might answer, yes, or He might answer, no. He might say maybe or He might say wait, but God will answer our prayers. And as you trust in Him, know that whatever the answer is, it will be sufficient.

Rev. Dr. Jasper Williams of Salem Bible Church in Atlanta, Georgia has said, "Pray and don't worry because when you have prayed you have done the best and the most that you can do. Just so He knows, and as long as He knows your heart things will work out." My favorite scripture in the Bible points this out: "And we know that all things work together for good to them that love God, to them who are the called according to his purpose." (Romans 8:28) Believe me when I tell you that prayer is a key to abundant living.

Allow me to share with you a story about prayer. I tell it every chance I get because of how it points to the power of prayer. Whether it is true or not, I do not know, but it is one of my favorite stories of all times. There was an old lady who lived in Central Alabama back in the early 50's. I knew her only as Aunt Mae. An elderly lady, Aunt Mae could not read, write nor count money. However, she was a devout Christian lady who had lived a very good life. Her only means of making a living had been domestic work in the homes of people. They had taken good care of her. One day she received a letter from her son who lived in Chicago. Aunt Mae took the letter to work and her friend and employer read the letter to her: "Mama, I hope this letter finds you in the best of health and strength. Unfortunately, I am not doing well at all. At a last visit to the doctor, he suggested that I contact my family as I may not have long to live. You being my only kin, I thought I would write and ask if you would come see me and be with me one final time. If you can't do this I certainly understand and simply ask that you keep me in your prayers and know that I love you dearly. You have been a great mama and I shall cherish our memories into eternity."

When Aunt Mae heard the news, she immediately asked her employer to help her to go see her son. Much to Aunt Mae's surprise, her employer's reply was negative. "Mae, you can't go to Chicago. You can't read or write; you might get lost. Mae, you can't go. Who'll take care of me and clean my house if you go?" Aunt Mae said, "Well, I'll go home and ask the Lord about this." She went home that afternoon, got down on her knees, and began to pray about her desire to be with her son.

"Now Lord, now, my Master … It's me Lord, knee bent and body bowed to the earth. I'm calling on your name asking you to please bless my son in his infirmities. If it be your will, let my son live, and spare me also just one more chance to see him and be with him just one more time. Lord, I can't read or write and have no money to pay for such a trip, but you've made a way for me time and time again. I'm asking you Master to grant me this one request." Aunt Mae prayed this prayer all through the night, and early in the morning, she felt compelled to pack her suitcase, to walk down to the train station, and to get on the train headed for Chicago. And that is exactly what she did. With a suitcase, a sack lunch, and a prayer in her heart she went down to the train station. She asked a man which train would take her to Chicago. When the man pointed her to that train, she went and boarded it.

As the train pulled off, the conductor came along and began to say to the passengers: "It's time to collect your fare or ticket for this trip". When he got to Aunt Mae, he asked for her fare. Her reply was, "I don't have any money, and I don't have no ticket but I want to see my son in Chicago." The conductor responded, "Why would you get on this train without a ticket?" Aunt Mae replied, "The Lord told me to get on this train." The Conductor was outraged. "Old lady, you are breaking the law and I could have you arrested. But if you don't have no ticket, I've got to put you off this train." The Conductor pulled the brake switch and the train stopped. The Conductor and his assistant took Aunt Mae and set her off the train.

Now when her feet touched the ground, Aunt Mae went right down on her knees and began to pray, "Lord, you told me to get on this train. Help me, Lord, in my time of need. I don't have nobody but you. Please have mercy on me ..." About this time, the Engineer called back to the Conductor and asked, "What's going on back there; why did you stop this train?" The Conductor replied, "Everything's ok, now. We had an old lady that I had to put off the train. She didn't have her ticket and refused to pay. Let's get rolling again." The Engineer released the brakes, busted up the engine, loosed the steam, and turned the switch, but the train would not move. He tried it again. He released the brakes, busted up the engine, loosed the steam, and turned the switch, but the train simply would not move. The Engineer called back to the Conductor again and said, "Something's wrong; this train will not move. What did you say happened?" The Conductor said, "Nothing really happened. I just put that old lady off the train as policy requires when they try to sneak on the train and ride without money or fare." "Well, what is that old lady doing", asked the Engineer? "She is out there on her knees mumbling. I guess she's praying or something but praying won't help her if she don't have no money," was the Conductor's reply. The Engineer was speechless and really did not know what to do but he replied, "Well, you better get that old lady and put her back on this train." Then, the Conductor and his assistant went out, picked Aunt Mae up, and put her back on the train. When Aunt Mae got to her seat, she told the Conductor, "I told you the Lord told me to get on this train."

And to everybody's surprise but Aunt Mae's, the Engineer released the brakes, busted up the engine, loosed the steam, turned the switch and that train begin to roll on down the track. This really had the Conductor upset with Aunt Mae. He said, "Aunt Mae, you think you're so smart. This train only goes to Detroit and you're trying to get to Chicago. When we get to Detroit, what are you going to do?" Aunt Mae answered, "Never you mind. The same God that told me to get on this train will get me to Chicago." The Conductor shook his head, walked away and never bothered Aunt Mae again. By the time the train reached Detroit, the other passengers on the train had pitched in together and had raised enough money to get Aunt Mae to Chicago and back home with money to spare. Now, I'm not suggesting anyone try something like this (unless directly told of the Lord to do so), but I hope you get the point. When you walk close to God, you can call on Him and He will hear your prayers and do for you things you never thought could happen. Prayer is a key to abundant living.

Finally, look at Jesus, the son of God. Of all his sayings and of all the things He did, the one example that stands above all others is that He was always praying. Before He performed miracles, He prayed. Oftentimes, He would get up early in the morning and in solitude, away from His disciples and anything else that could distract Him, He prayed. In His darkest hour there in the Garden of Gethsemane, He prayed. Even on the cross, He prayed. It was so important to Him for us to pray as He taught us to pray in that portion of scripture we call, "The Model Prayer." The Bible makes it clear that our Lord and Savior was a praying Son. He made sure that He stayed in the presence of His Father by way of prayer. Now, if Jesus was persistent and consistent in His prayer life, we should certainly follow His example. Abundant living is achieved when we keep our lives, our loved ones, and those in the community we share with bathed in prayer. It is a power source like none other.

Step IV:
True Love Also Means Forgiving

I believe nothing hinders our lives more from being fulfilled, peaceful, and fun than living in this world with grudges and vengefulness in our minds and our hearts against our fellow man. Think about it. Being angry longer than a few hours begins to tear away at our soul like a sickness. It literally paralyzes us from doing anything positive. I may not be able to help the fact that someone might consider me his enemy, but my philosophy of relationships is to always strive to be a friend to mankind. It is healthier. It is most pleasant, and it helps others with whom we interact. An old adage states, "It takes less muscles and energy to smile than to frown."

My dad died on January 1, 2004. He was 74 years old. I saw my dad only a few times in my life. Each time it was by my visiting him. I believe he loved me and cared for me, but because of his past relationship with my mother, he somehow never pursued a real relationship with me. We talked often on the phone for long periods of time. Then, at times, we would quarrel and not talk for years. It was a sad situation. However, I never gave up on my dad. I would talk to him about the Lord. I would encourage him to seek the Lord and be saved. I would share with him the ups and downs of rearing my children. My wife and I would visit him and send pictures and I would call him most holidays just to say hello and to let him know that I loved him. He was mostly mum to all of this though I did not hold this against him. I just charged it to his head, but not to his heart. At least that is what I thought. My father's death came as a surprise. My brother brought him to our hometown for his funeral and final resting place. In doing that, it became my honor to eulogize my father. To the best of my ability, I spoke of only fond memories and of hope for our future together with the Lord in Heaven.

I was surprised to know that he had left an inheritance for his family. However, when I found out that I (nor any of my children) were left anything, I was devastated. I am not greedy, nor do I think I am covetous of what others have. I simply resented the fact that my dad thought so little of my family and me that he left us nothing. I became a bitter, hurt man, and finally resented him. Isn't that something? I had spent all my life trying to be his son, his friend. I had asked very little of him. Now, I was insulted and humiliated. I was his oldest child. Being a minister, I, too, had financial needs just like my other two brothers. However, he did not remember me with anything. I did not hate him for how he treated me, but something not of God did emerge in my spirit. For months, I was not at peace. I remembered how I had often told him that I wanted nothing from him but friendship, but when he left me out of his will, I was devastated. This devastation and resentment lasted for months until finally I realized that my dad was dead and I was not hurting anyone but myself. It was also at this time that God allowed me to see how blessed I was with my own family. We all have good health and strength. My wife is happy and fulfilled in her work, and my children are doing fine in their lives. I am blessed to be a pastor at a church working to do God's will. I thought of how good the congregation has been to me down through the years. Then I thought of how my Heavenly Father has been so good to me. The truth is all of my life my needs and desires had been met more than I could have ever expected. I have been blessed all of my life by God, family, and friends. Why would I make money an issue now? Therefore, I knew I had to fall on my knees and ask the Lord to forgive me for harboring anything against my dad.

There is one thing I have come to realize about asking God for forgiveness. Some issues take time to heal and to allow us to completely let go. This was my case with my dad. As the days passed, I would again think of how I felt about what my dad had done. I would say or think, "It is OK", or "Everything is going to be all right." Then I would immediately move on to something else. Then something came to mind that I had (maybe subconsciously) buried for years. When I was perhaps 26 or 27 years old, my father called and asked me to change my name. He told me that he wanted me to change my name so that he could leave me something in the event of his death. As we talked that day, I thought about it. I thought about the fact that I had a wife and children who bore my name. The sign in front of the church where I was Pastor at the time had my name on it, Carey N. Ingram. At the end of the conversation, I told him that I would not change my name. All of my family and close friends knew my situation of having been born out of wedlock. It was never an issue. I am very close to my Perkins family.

About a week later, he called again and asked me to change my name. He wanted me to change my name privately, which meant to change it legally, but simply not make it public. Again, I thought and decided I could not be Carey

Perkins and my family have the last name of Ingram. I made it clear to him that if he wanted to leave me something, he could leave it in my present name. Carey Nathaniel Ingram is who I was from birth. For whatever good I had done, for all that I stood for had been identified with my name. I was not going to change it. My dad made it clear that if I would not change my name, he could not leave me any part of his inheritance.

Was there too much pride on both our parts? Was I acting immature? Was he finally trying to reach out to me? Was he asking too much of me at that time in my life? Truly, the answer is blowing in the wind. When I recalled this situation that had been buried in my heart for almost 25 years, two important points came to mind. First, my father did not leave me out of his inheritance out of malice. I was just as responsible for that situation as he was. He offered me an inheritance that I chose not to be a part of. Second, I see clearer the kind of man my father was. He was a man of his word, and it was that day that I finally got the release that I needed to move forward from negative feelings about my father.

My dad did what he thought was best, what he was led to do. So again, I asked God to forgive me and I asked my dad to forgive me. Then I forgave myself and put it behind me. Now I deal with nothing but the warm and positive memories of my dad. Now, I can tell you how proud I am that this man was my father because I have his genes in me. Because he was who he was, I am who I am. My looks, my demeanor, my intellect, my articulation, my drive, my personality and my instincts are a result of what my mother and father both gave me in their genes. I would have loved to have been brought up in a home where they reared me, but that was not God's will. One thing I do know is that I am not a mistake. I have tried to make a difference in this world. My father owes me nothing; rather, I am indebted to both my parents for bringing me into this world.

I am determined never again to let money or what I think I deserve hinder me from being the best person I can be. I know now that the best I can be is God's child and He will take care of all my needs if I trust Him. Sometimes I believe God allows certain things to happen in our lives to see if we believe and trust Him as we say we do. For the most part, I have always been a forgiving person. I must admit that was one time I failed terribly. I shall work harder so that nothing like this ever happens again in my life.

In the final analysis, is not all of life about relationships? I have developed over the years an order for my life that keeps me feeling good about living. First, I daily re-establish my relationship with my God. Second, I reinforce my love and feeling toward my immediate family. Third, I try very hard to give my best side (behavior, attitude, and friendship) to those with whom I come into contact on a daily basis. And it is important that I do those things in that order. Now, the key element to making that happen is my ability to approach relationships with love.

My simple and general definition of love is a passion from the heart that drives me to do what I believe is right and good for the sake of all those around me, and to ask for nothing in return. It is, indeed, a love that comes from my relationship with God; therefore, I can't help myself when it comes to loving mankind. It is more than just feelings and emotions. Rather, it is my character born out of my desire to be like the God that made me. Love is the key to relationships. I do not confess to love everybody the same, but there is a love that comes from God that allows me to meet each person where he is. Love is the greatest gift of character that God gives us. In 1 Corinthians 13:13, the apostle sets forth the excellence of love as the word, "charity". "And now abideth faith, hope, charity, these three; but the greatest of these is charity." Here is what Jesus told John about love: "A new commandment I give unto you, that ye love one another; as I have loved you, that ye also love one another. By this shall all men know that ye are my disciples, if ye have love one to another. (1 John 13:34-35) Listen to what John, the beloved of Jesus, says about love: "No man hath seen God at any time. If we love one another, God dwelleth in us, and his love is perfected in us". (1 John 4:12) "And we have known and believed the love that God hath to us. God is love; and he that dwelleth in love dwelleth in God, and God in him." (1 John 4:16) "If a man say, I love God, and hateth his brother, he is a liar: for he that loveth not his brother whom he hath seen, how can he love God whom he hath not seen?"(1 John 4:20) "For this is the love of God, that we keep his commandments: and his commandments are not grievous." (1 John 5:3)

At the Lovejoy Baptist Church where I serve as Senior Pastor, we have adopted a policy of saying to one another, "I love You," and the congregation responds with the same. Over a period of time, I noticed that the response was faint. I came to realize that not everyone in the congregation loves everyone else. I have taken the time to teach and share lessons on the importance of love. The gist of my appeal to the congregation is for them to realize that if we do not love one another, then we can never reach lost souls for Christ because the way you reach the lost for Christ is with love. I concluded by sharing another profound scripture on love:

> "Though I speak with the tongues of men and of angels, and have not charity, I am become as sounding brass, or a tinkling cymbal. And though I have the gift of prophecy, and understand all mysteries, and all knowledge; and though I have all faith, so that I could remove mountains, and have not charity, I am nothing. And though I bestow all my goods to feed the poor, and

though I give my body to be burned, and have not charity, it profiteth me nothing."(1 Corinthians 13:1-3)

It was then that I found out that in order to really love people with God's love, you have to also be willing to forgive one another. Yes, I have discovered that many people (yes, church people) are trying to worship God and serve God with the weight of unforgiveness in their hearts. If you really desire to live an abundant life, then you must be willing to forgive.

In the book of Matthew, we find these words: "Then came Peter to him, and said, Lord, how oft shall my brother sin against me, and I forgive him? Till seven times? Jesus saith unto him, I say not unto thee, until seven times: but, until seventy times seven."(Matthew 18:21-22)

The Lord had just spoken of the duty of seeking reconciliation with those who trespass against us:

"Moreover if thy brother shall trespass against thee, go and tell him his fault between thee and him alone: if he shall hear thee, thou hast gained thy brother. But if he will not hear thee, then take with thee one or two more, that in the mouth of two or three witnesses every word may be established."(Matthew 18:15-17)

Now there seems to have been some doubt in the mind of Peter as to how far this principle should be carried. Till seven times? It is stated that the Jewish Rabbis held that forgiveness must be extended to one who confessed his fault, but this was limited to three repetitions of the offense. Peter had an idea that the Savior's rule would insist on still greater forbearance. So that is when Jesus replied unto him, "I say not unto thee, until seven times: but, until seventy times seven." This really means as often as you need to forgive others, that is how often you should forgive. Forgiving others not only sets them free, but it sets you free to move forward with the life God has for you.

True love is never present until we have sought reconciliation with those who trespass against us. To do that, we must become familiar with what it really means to forgive. Let me show you how infrequently we practice forgiveness in our lives. I can do that by asking you, when was the last time you asked anybody to forgive you? On the other hand, when was the last time you said to anyone: I am sorry; let's start all over again. If you are honest about it, we very seldom practice forgiveness. The obvious question is: What does it mean to forgive? The Old Testament defines forgiveness as the sense of removal of sin and restoration of the relationship, which was damaged by sin. In all cases, forgiveness requires a change of heart and mind. Unfortunately, animals do better at forgiving than we as God's crown creation.

Dale Carnegie tells this story: There is not a meaner or more ferocious beast in the wild than the grizzly bear; yet the skunk has no fear of him. You see both of them have had a change of heart. The grizzly bear knows that he can tear a skunk into shreds; yet, he also knows that the skunk with one spray of his scent can make his life miserable long after his death. So they compromise; they respect each other's gifts and talents and some times side by side, they scrounge around for food. If only we can be like the skunk and the grizzly bear.

Carnegie says bitterness, grudge bearing, and vengefulness are the most dangerous of all plagues to healthy Christian living. It will eat away at the vitality of your spiritual life until your once vibrant testimony is in shambles. It is the "cancer of the soul", and it claims millions of victims each year. It spreads faster than the common cold and threatens the survival of many churches.

Let us consider three kinds of forgiveness. The first is PATERNAL FORGIVENESS. This has to do with the believer's fellowship with God and is most important for how can we be Christian in nature if we are not in fellowship with God? As our relationship goes better with God, it also goes better with others. The Bible tells us our problem. We are weak and by nature, we are self-centered. We err, are prone to make mistakes, and are all born and shaped in iniquity. Therefore, we must constantly strive to be God-centered. Now as Christians, we are saved, and we belong to God, but that does not guarantee fellowship or the right relationship with Him. Salvation is a gift from God, through Jesus Christ, but discipleship and fellowship with God is something we must constantly work toward. We can achieve this goal by humble submission and confession to Him in prayer asking for forgiveness of our shortcomings. Otherwise, fellowship with God is broken by continued, unconfessed sin. That is why everyday as God allows us to wake into this world and to lie down at night, we should go to God in prayer confessing our sins and making our peace with Him. Our relationship with God is the key to a blessed life, a victorious life, and a life of servitude. The songwriter says, "Oh what peace we often forfeit, oh what needless pain we bear; all because we do not carry everything to God in prayer." Paternal forgiveness is cleansing, purging, and imperative if one wants to experience liberation and freedom in Christ. Otherwise, one walks around in this world with the weight of his unforgiven sins. This leads to sickness, depression, and paranoia because we are not in the right relationship with God.

The second type of forgiveness is PERSONAL FORGIVENESS. This forgiveness is a restoration of fellowship with another human being. This facet of forgiveness is so important that Jesus conditions our forgiveness and restoration to fellowship with our Heavenly Father on our willingness to forgive others. Let us look at this idea in what we call the "Model Prayer" that Jesus gave us:

> "And forgive us our debts, as we forgive our debtors. And lead us not into temptation, but deliver us from evil: For Thine is the kingdom, and the power, and the glory, forever. Amen. For if ye forgive men their trespasses, your heavenly Father will also forgive you …"(Matthew 6:12-14)

Why is forgiveness so important? Jesus gives us an answer and a startling warning. If we refuse to forgive others, God will refuse to forgive us. Why? Because when we do not forgive others, we are denying our common ground as sinners in need of God's mercy. How can we dare not forgive others and have the nerve to humbly go before God to ask for the same. The truth is we can do nothing to please God if we are not in fellowship with our fellow man. Let me show you in scripture again just how dangerous it is to not be in fellowship with your fellow man:

> "For I say unto you, That except your righteousness shall exceed the righteousness of the scribes and Pharisees, ye shall in no case enter into the kingdom of heaven. Ye have heard that it was said by them of old time, Thou shalt not kill; and whosoever shall kill shall be in danger of the judgment: But I say unto you, That whosoever is angry with his brother without a cause shall be in danger of the judgment: and whosoever shall say to his brother, Raca, shall be in danger of the council: but whosoever shall say, Thou fool, shall be in danger of hell fire. Therefore, if thou bring thy gift to the altar, and there rememberest that thy brother hath ought against thee; Leave there thy gift before the altar, and go thy way; first be reconciled to thy brother, and then come and offer thy gift."(Matthew 5:20-24)

He says it again in Mark: "And when ye stand praying, forgive, if ye have ought against any: that your Father also which is in heaven may forgive you your trespasses."(Mark 11:25)

All I am trying to convey to you is that we who profess to be Christians must be loving, kind, and forgiving. Why? The very basis of Christianity is based upon loving one another, being kind to one another, and forgiving one another. Listen to what Paul said to the church of Ephesus: "And be ye kind one to another, tenderhearted, forgiving one another, even as God for Christ's sake hath forgiven you."(Ephesians 4:23) Why forgive? Because forgiveness is God's way. Grudge bearing is the devil's way. The world says, "If you hit me, I'm going to hit you back." But, if you are going to live for God, you must be willing to say and do that which seems strange to the world. You must be willing when people take from you to give. When people hate, you must love; when others abuse, you must help. Yes, it is all about giving up your right for the wrong and sometimes knowing well that when God gets ready, He will bring His righteousness and His judgment to all of us. People might be getting by right now, but none of us can escape God. God is loving and kind, but do not ever forget that God has a wrath; that is to say, God has a belt and when he gets ready, He will tear on the hide of those who deserve it.

How many homes could have been saved if there had been forgiveness in the house? How many marriages could have been saved if someone had said, "I'm sorry" and the other partner had accepted? How many friendships could have been saved? How many wars could have been avoided? How many problems could have been solved if only someone with the love of God had said, "Forgive me and let's start all over again." Forgiveness should be a way of life for the children of God. You have got to do it, and mean it from your heart.

Do not be like JOHN and LEWIS. These two men were lifelong friends; they went to school together and lived side by side with their families. They went on outings, picnics, fishing trips, and always enjoyed each other's company. Over a simple matter of John not giving Lewis the correct amount of change from a grocery store visit, they became bitter enemies. For years they did not speak. They would sit on their respective porches and never look toward each other. One day John fell sick and it appeared life threatening. After much thought, Lewis decided it was time to go to John and to make his peace. When Lewis entered the house, they began to talk and seemed to be forgiving of one another; yet, as the conversation continued, they came back to the few dollars that had caused the end of the friendship to start with. Believe it or not, Lewis left angry with John again and a few days later, John died and they never had a chance to make their peace. Can you imagine that? Yet, it happens all the time. People, for whatever the reason, refuse to let go and let the love of God prevail in those unfortunate ugly circumstances. I hope and pray that never happens again in my life or yours.

The third and final type of forgiveness is JUDICIAL FORGIVENESS. This is eternal forgiveness of all sins of the one who has trusted Christ. This goes with the doctrine of justification and has to do with the believer's relationship with God. It is not enough for you to ask God to forgive you. It is not enough for you to forgive others, but you also have to forgive yourself. Are you suffering because you have done everything God has required except to forgive yourself? It does not matter what it is. Maybe you broke up a marriage, hurt a child, abused a wife, stole from your job, or caused someone's tragic fall. God says that when you get ready, you can let it go. Just ask Him to forgive you; forgive yourself, and then start all over again. Keep this in mind: With God you can always start over again.

John states: "If we confess our sins, he is faithful and just to forgive us our sins, and to cleanse us from all unrighteousness."(I John 1:9) Some self-righteous Christians, who are in trouble themselves, do not like the fact that as long as you live, you are prone to sin. As long as we live in this world in our flesh, we are subject to sin, but as often as you ask God through Jesus to forgive you, He will. That was his point to Peter. Jesus is saying as often as I have to pick you up, turn you around, place your feet on solid ground, I will. The Psalmist declares: "As far as the east is from the west, so far hath he removed our transgressions from us. Like as a father pitieth his children, so the LORD pitieth them that fear him. For he knoweth our frame; he remembereth that we are dust."(Psalm 103:12-14)

Be not dismayed. When Jesus went to the cross, He died that we might be forgiven of all sin. All He needs is for us to ask. To carry the guilt of sin will surely weigh you down. If you are unhappy, you will make the people around you miserable. Singers cannot sing right, deacons cannot bow and pray right, workers will not work, and Preachers cannot preach with power when sin is weighing them down.

Therefore, I am asking you today if there is anybody in your life somewhere with whom you need to make your peace, do it now or as soon as you can and be set free. And if by chance they will not accept your apology, then give that to God and go on and live your life. All you can do is ask. You cannot make people forgive you.

In concluding this chapter, I want you to know that there are a lot of hurting people in the world, and we who know better have to tell them that there is hope in asking God for forgiveness.

There is a story of a boy named Pacos who never had a good relationship with his father. They both tried to get along, but as he grew to be a teenager, he became more and more rebellious, particularly against his father. One day after an intense argument, Pacos left home. Only sixteen, he was a lad out of control, and on his own roaming the streets and countryside of Mexico. After he had been away from home for a couple of months, it was more than his mother and father could stand. His dad wept openly and went out day and night looking for his son. He left word everywhere that if anyone should see his son, to tell him his father said all is forgiven and to please come home. Pacos' dad had exhausted all he knew to do to find his son. His final attempt to locate him was to put an announcement in all the surrounding newspapers asking for his son to come to the newspaper company in this little Mexican town of Halo at noon on Saturday. It is said that on that Saturday over 12 hundred men and boys showed up in response to that announcement.

Yes, people are hurting and looking for reconciliation with God, their fellow-man and with themselves. I don't know about you, but I have made up in my mind that I am going to work at relationships until I get it right. There is no greater power than love and forgiveness. It is my prayer that God will grant that power to work in my life.

Step V:
Struggles Are Just A Test

When I was around seven or eight, one of my favorite times was Saturday morning and watching television. I enjoyed Mighty Mouse, Heckle and Jeckle, Flipper, My Friend, Flicka, The Lone Ranger, Looney Tune Cartoons, and the list goes on and on. From about 8:00 a.m. until well past noon, my brother and I would be glued to the television. I remember during this time, at some point, one of the programs would be interrupted with what I came to realized was a standard test of the emergency broadcast system. The television screen would turn blue with an emblem of an Indian image and an announcer would say, "This is a test of the emergency broadcasting system." Now for about thirty seconds you would hear a sound like a dull siren as this test was being conducted. Then the announcer would come back and say, "This was only a test. If this had been an actual emergency, you would have been given further instructions through this broadcasting network. Stay tuned for your regular scheduled programs."

That has stayed with me all of my life and now I know why. I have come to realize that much of the struggles we go through in life are only tests. Have you ever thought that there are really no emergencies in Heaven? There is nothing on earth that spooks or startles God or causes Him to say, "OH, MY GOD." Since, as a Christian, I am under God's arc of safety, then I have no real emergencies either.

The Apostle Peter wrote a letter to encourage believers who were facing trials and persecution under Emperor Nero of Rome. During most of the first century, Christians were hunted down and killed throughout the Roman Empire. They suffered social and economic persecution from three main sources: the Romans, the Jews, and their own families. Some were misunderstood; others were harassed and a few were tortured and even put to death. Peter was telling the people to look to Christ:

> "Blessed be the God and Father of our Lord Jesus Christ, which according to his abundant mercy hath begotten us again unto a lively hope by the resur-

rection of Jesus Christ from the dead, To an inheritance incorruptible, and undefiled, and that fadeth not away, reserved in heaven for you, Who are kept by the power of God through faith unto salvation ready to be revealed in the last time." (1 Peter1: 3-5)

Peter's words offer joy and hope in times of trouble, and he bases his confidence on what God has done for us in Christ Jesus. Over the years, I have learned this valuable lesson that helps me in my time of struggles: when problems come, we must focus on Jesus and not the problem. Why Jesus? Well, Hebrews declares: "Looking unto Jesus the author and finisher of our faith; who for the joy that was set before him endured the cross, despising the shame, and is set down at the right hand of the throne of God." (Hebrews 12:2)

So we do not need to panic, or to fear because the Father and Son are together and in charge of everything in the heavens and the earth. The Holy Spirit is also present with us as our comforter, teacher, and guide. What we are experiencing is just a Test! Satan is never going to leave us alone. Therefore, temptations will come, and every now and then, God will allow trials and tribulations to come our way because he wants to see us grow in grace and to perfect His will in our lives, for our lives. Struggles in the form of temptations, trials, and tribulations are just tests. They are not emergencies.

The Grolier Encyclopedia says that tests are to determine ones abilities, achievements, and effectiveness. Tests are used to select people for special instruction and particular jobs. Therefore, when on those days that your bubble is about to burst; when you have just used all your money paying your bills, and your car breaks down; when you need an extra $350 so you can get the car fixed to get to work, or you have done all you can with that child and for that child, but he or she will not act right and ends up in a court of law, remember, it is just a test. When you have labored in your home for years and years, and in spite of all you do, your husband does not seem to appreciate you and, as a matter of fact, has been criticizing you lately for minor things, do not let those kinds of things get you down. It is only a test. Remember you are going to have some good days, but you are also going to have some bad days, too. With any test, you have to go through the process in order to get the desired results. Let us hear James's perspective on this: "My brethren, count it all joy when ye fall into diver's temptation; knowing this, that the trying of your faith worketh patience. But let patience have her perfect work, that ye may be perfect and entire, wanting nothing." (James 1: 2-4)

The word temptation as used here refers to trials or testing. It does not mean an enticement to do evil. While God does test us, he never provokes us to sin. Notice that James does not say *if* we face trials, but *when* we face trials. He assumes we will have trials and that it is possible to profit from them. We are not required to pretend to be happy when we face hurts and disappointments, but we need to have a positive outlook because of the results trials and tribulations will bring. James tells us to turn our hardships into times of learning. Rough times can teach us patience and we can never know the depth of our character until we see how we react under pressure. When God lets us go through things, he is making us mature and complete. It is just a test. We can say many great things about those in the Bible who have taken these tests.

When we consider tests, Job comes to mind: The bible declares Job to be "perfect" and "upright", a man that feared God and eschewed evil. When Satan came into the presence of God, He asked Satan, "Hast thou considered my servant Job?" Satan said, "Look at how good you've been to him, and how you have that hedge around him. Move the hedge and touch his possession and he will curse thee to thy face." God's response was: "All that he hath is in thy power, only upon himself put not forth Thine hand." Satan went and literally took away everything that Job possessed. (Read Job1:8, 13-22). Now when Satan stood before God again, God again asked him: "Have you considered my servant Job? All that I have allowed you to do to him without cause." Satan's reply was "Skin for Skin, yea, all that a man hath will he give for his life. Touch his flesh and bone, and he will curse thee." So, God allowed Satan to touch his life, but he could not take his life which is to say he could not touch his soul. Satan went away and smote Job with sore boils from the crown of his head to the sole of his feet. Now look at Job's answer to all his suffering: "But he said unto her, Thou speakest as one of the foolish women speaketh. What? Shall we receive good at the hand of God, and shall we not receive evil? In all this did not Job sin with his lips?"(Job 2:10) Job must have realized that what he was experiencing was only a Test! Job's ultimate response to his troubles was, "Yet though he slay me, still will I trust him." (Job 13:15)

Abraham is called the Father of the Faith, and he had to face a test in order to be who God truly wanted him to be. God had promised Abraham and Sara that he would multiply their seed and that their number would equal the grains of sand. The only problem is God made this promise when both were in their old age. Sara was 99 and Abraham was 100 years old. Yet, God kept his word and they had a son named Isaac. Now words cannot express how happy they were to have this son, and remember, it would be through Isaac that Abraham's seed would flourish. Look at the book of Genesis: "And it came to pass after these things, that God did tempt Abraham, and said unto him, Abraham: and he said, Behold, here I am." (Genesis 22:1) The temptation is a test to see if Abraham would be faithful in executing what God asked of him. God simply wanted to know if Abraham loved the gift (his son) more than he loved the one who gave him the gift (God). In verse 12 of this passage, we see that God told Abraham, "You are indeed my servant who fears and reverence me." And, Abraham was blessed because he was able to grow from this experience. God knows that in life we are going to be tested.

Now, we should rejoice in knowing that we are going to be tested because we see from two examples that tests bring testimonies which tell the world that you are a witness about the Goodness of God, and therefore when trouble arises in your life, you can rejoice and thank God that he would use you.

Lives are full of struggles, but just remember if we belong to Christ, struggles can be overcome. Struggles are just tests! This means we are blessed to grow and become seasoned in the faith. We enjoy the sunshine, appreciate the rain, and enjoy the summer time, but we also live well in the winter season. We learn how to stand in the calm and in the storm as well.

A man tells the story of how he raised a palm tree in New Orleans, how he loved it and nurtured it for years and years. However, the palm tree can only endure so much cold weather or it will easily die. As it would be, there was a cold winter in New Orleans one year and the palm tree died. The man, however, could look at the oak tree on the other side of his yard. He said, "That oak tree was here when I moved here, and I suspect that tree is more than 100 years old. No matter how hot or cold, through windstorms and hard rains, that old oak tree still stands." A palm tree may be pretty, but an oak tree can live and deal with all seasons of life. So, it is for those who walk through life with Christ.

I am reminded of the preacher who talked about how he would go jogging for blocks every morning, and at this one block, one of his neighbor's dog would always startle him. It was a huge dog, a Great Dane, which would always run toward him barking as he ran past. The man ran this route every morning; yet, he would somehow always forget that the huge dog was waiting to scare him. Now, the reason why the dog only barked and scared him, never grabbed or even bit him is because the dog was in his yard, locked behind a fence. The dog would jump and growl, run and bark, but that is all he could do. He was always frightening the jogger, but he could never harm him because he was locked within the gates. That reminds me of the scripture that lets me know who I am. Jesus says in Matthew 16:18, "Upon this rock I will build my church and the gates of hell shall not prevail against it". Satan will try to scare you, bark at you, chase you, run you down, but he is in the gate and the gates of hell shall not prevail against you. The devil will come at you with all his evil, but God will turn it for your good. Listen to how eloquently Isaiah explains this: "No weapon that is formed against thee shall prosper; and every tongue that shall rise against thee in judgment thou shalt condemn. This is the heritage of the servants of the LORD, and their righteousness is of me, saith the LORD." (Isaiah 54:17)

This idea brings up a lot of questions. How do I deal with my struggles? How do I pass my test? What do I do when everything seems so unbearable? What do we do when we have done all we know to do in our times of struggle? I want to recommend two things that will help you to endure during your time of effort. Number one, Count It All Joy. Number two, Hold Your Hope.

Know this: Trials are universal; they are just as much a part of life as anything else. Satan tempts us and God will send trials into our lives. We are always coming out, going through, or getting ready to go through some kind of circumstance or situation. Sometimes it is good; sometimes it is troublesome. Again, I choose to call it the adventures of life. It is almost impossible to have relationships with people and not get hurt or hurt someone at some point. You can be well intended yet your good intentions can be so drastically misunderstood. Left alone to face life, these troubles can cause some people to drop off the scene. They simply withdraw from life and live beneath their privileges because they refuse to go through the storms and fires set before them. We must learn to master our trials or our trials will master us. How, then, do we endure our trials and temptations? James gives us the answer:

> "My brethren, count it all joy when ye fall into divers temptations; Knowing this, that the trying of your faith worketh patience. But, let patience have her perfect work, that ye may be perfect and entire, wanting nothing. If any of you lack wisdom, let him ask of God, that giveth to all men liberally, and upbraideth not; and it shall be given him. But, let him ask in faith, nothing wavering. For he that wavereth is like a wave of the sea driven with the wind and tossed." (James 1:2-6)

James said, "Count It All Joy." That means that whatever you are going through, consider it a calm delight. As Jesus was about to begin His trial and tribulation ministry, listen to what He said to his disciples to encourage them: "These things I have spoken unto you, that in me ye might have peace. In the world ye shall have tribulation: but be of good cheer; I have overcome the world." (John 16:33)

This is a direct statement from Jesus that we will have trials and tribulations, but we are to rejoice about it. It is the Christian way because Christianity must not only be believed, it must also be lived. I heard a preacher say that tests come to mellow us. Like marinating meat, it takes time, but it adds flavor. Tests come to shake us out of our spiritual ruts, to move us to pray and to keep the promises we made. Through tests, we are taught to practice what we preach. Finally, he said that tests come to perfect us. This is an ongoing process that leads to Christian maturity. God is not trying to make us happy, but rather to make us Holy. When we are Holy, we are mature, set up to do that which we are called to do—to do that which only we can do. This is why we "Count It All Joy." If we persevere to the end of temptations, trials, and tribulations, then we become exactly who Christ would have us to be. Remember, tests are only temporary; tests are tabulated. God knows just how much we can bear. Tests are therapeutic; they do not come to make us bitter; they come to make us better. "Count it all joy." Thank God, I know he will not put any more on you than you are able to bear. He will be with you even until the end. He will help you through your struggles.

It was one of my daily devotional readings that gave me the second answer I was looking for. The topic was entitled, "A Living Hope." It began by saying that life is hard for everyone. It is harder for some than it is for others. In fact, I want to go on record as saying that life is not fair. One child is born to royalty and never has to worry about a proper place in society or what money can buy. Yet, another child is born to a single parent and rival siblings and some days there is not enough food to go around. There is nothing in the Bible that promises us a free pass from trials and tribulation just because we follow Christ. In fact, some problems intensify when we make that decision to live for the Lord. Have you, like me, been a tither, yet sometimes your money seems to come up short? We rear our children the best we can, trying to get them through college with hopes that they can make a decent living for themselves. Yet, some guys grow up with no schooling, but learn how to rap and curse, and call people out of their names and become millionaires. Some folk love the Lord and get close to Him, yet they have to live with a sickness that burdens them all their lives. Some people have children for whom they do everything, yet they end up going astray. Some spouses work hard to make the marriage work while others seem less and less interested. Many try their best to live for the Lord, but then seem not to be able to rid themselves of personal demons. Those bad habits die down; then they rise up again and they feel like hypocrites. Life can be so hard. Many get down and depressed. If you take one step forward, then the devil knocks you two steps back. It is enough to make you throw up you hands in surrender.

However, I want to remind you, today, that whatever you are up against or going through: Hold Your Hope. You are not alone. Yes, life is full of struggles. The scripture teaches us: "Man that is born of a woman is of few days, and full of trouble." (Job 14:1) God never promised us that the Christian journey would always be smooth and easy. In fact, Jesus said, "If any man will come after me, let him deny himself, and take up his cross and follow me." (Luke 9:23)

The good part is that God himself never leaves us and always has something in place to help us through all our trials, tribulations, and adversities. One of these virtues is Hope. Hope must be embedded in Christian Character. The Eastman Bible Dictionary defines hope as one of the three main elements of Christian character. (1 Corinthians 13:13) It is joined to faith and love, and is opposed to seeing or possessing. In other words, if you can see your way out or work things out yourself, you do not need hope. It is one of those things that separate us from the rest of the world. Unbelievers are without this hope. (Ephesians 2:12; 1 Thessalonians 4:13) Christ is the actual object of the believer's hope because it is in his Second Coming that the hope of glory will be fulfilled. (1 Timothy 1:1; Colossians 1:27; Titus 2:13) It is spoken of as "lively", i.e., a living hope, a hope not frail and perishable, but having a perennial life. (1 Peter 1:3) How many times have you, like me, had those days when you could not help but wonder, why Lord, why is all of this happening to me? Sometimes it is sickness, sometimes it is finances, and sometimes it is problems in the home or on the job. And, while you are going through, it seems like it will never end. It seems as though there is not any relief in sight. You have done all you can do, and said all you can say. You have sought help where you could yet these bad things continue to flow like water flowing down a stream. You are at the point of hopelessness.

I have learned to never call a day "bad" until I have seen the whole day. My experience in my relationship with God is that, "He may not come when we want Him to, but He is always right on time." When I look back over my life, I must bear witness that through it all He has always heard my cry and given me not only consolation, but also the victory. Have you ever thought that maybe one of the reasons the Christian seems to have it so hard at times is because God is preparing us for the great work that lies ahead. Remember, in the First Chapter of Joshua, God is talking to Joshua about the fact that His servant Moses was now dead and Joshua was to take on the leadership role over all of Israel. It was now his task to lead them into the Promise Land. Within that one chapter God tells Joshua at least four times, "Be Strong and Of Good Courage." He declares unto Joshua that wherever your feet walk, "I'll walk with you." He did not promise him everything would go his way. He did not tell him that there would not be war or trouble within the camp. However, God did promise to be with him and that is what having hope is all about. It is the expectation that God is with us no matter what appears to be.

Whether it is fire, water, hurricanes, tornadoes, pestilence, or famine, Hope is saying that God not only cares, but also is very present in the midst of whatever you are going through. I wish I had time to share all the times God has revealed himself to me in or around my time of need. All I can say is that in my life when I have had crises or calamities or when life's problems seemed far over my head, I have found that when the dust settled, there stood God holding me in His arms and I was doing just fine.

Then, there is another angle that we must look at that may give reason as to why we sometimes have these feelings of hopelessness. A friend of mine shared this verse of scripture that blessed me and I need to share it with you. The verse reads: "Blessed is the man that endureth temptation: for when he is tried, he shall receive the crown of life, which the Lord hath promised to them that love him." (James 1:12) Don't ever forget the best is yet to come for those of us who love the Lord. Then the scripture defines part of our problem:

> "Let no man say when he is tempted, I am tempted of God: for God cannot be tempted with evil, neither tempteth he any man: But every man is tempted, when he is drawn away of his own lust, and enticed. Then when lust hath conceived, it bringeth forth sin: and sin, when it is finished, bringeth forth death. Do not err, my beloved brethren." (James 1:13-16)

Now, I want to share another story which a friend shared with me: A few friends were having lunch in a town square. From the window, they looked and saw across the street a homeless man who was holding up a sign that read, "I will work for food." The only things this man had were the clothes on his back, the sign, and a back pack. This man intrigued them all. People all over the restaurant and in the streets were drawn to this man, but never ventured toward him. After lunch, this one man, we will call David, was driving back to work and could not get the vision of this man out of his mind. Eventually, he circled back around and found him. He greeted this homeless man, we will call Daniel, and invited him to lunch. While Daniel ate, he shared with David that he was homeless by choice. Most of what was in his backpack were Bibles that he distributed to those with whom he often got involved. For 14 years, he had been homeless because he felt led by God to dedicate his life to sharing the Gospel of Jesus Christ in this manner. They continued to talk about their relationships with God as David was a Christian also. David offered Daniel money and invited him to stay in his home until he was rested. Daniel graciously refused both offers. All he asked of David was that every time he thought of him, to keep him in his prayers. When David took Daniel back to the town square area, they prayed together and went their separate ways. Daniel left a pair of gloves in David's car. Those gloves now sit on David's desk at work. Every time he notices those gloves, he prays for Daniel.

The point of the story is that life is simpler, less stressful, and most rewarding when our only aim is to please God. You might think that is an extreme example and I agree that the path that Daniel took in life is not for everybody, but remember that Daniel was compelled by God to live this life. What if we sought God and lived our lives seeking to please Him first? Most people miss this very important key to living life. A God-centered, God-led life does not necessarily mean you do not have fun or pleasure. In simple language, one puts seeking the Kingdom of God first. Daniel is the exception, not the rule. In fact, I know but only a few people who have been so dedicated. Look at the life of Jesus. Now, I am not suggesting for one minute that everyone live like that, but I am suggesting that the world would be better and we would be more hopeful if we didn't always think of the things of this world but of the world to come. And that is what Peter, like James, is conveying to us:

> "Blessed be the God and Father of our Lord Jesus Christ, which according to his abundant mercy hath begotten us again unto a lively hope by the resurrection of Jesus Christ from the dead, To an inheritance incorruptible, and undefiled, and that fadeth not away, reserved in heaven for you, Who are kept by the power of God through faith unto salvation ready to be revealed in the last time. Wherein ye greatly rejoice, though now for a season, if need be, ye are in heaviness through manifold temptations: That the trial of your faith, being much more precious than of gold that perisheth, though it be tried with fire, might be found unto praise and honour and glory at the appearing of Jesus Christ: Whom having not seen, ye love; in whom, though now ye see him not, yet believing, ye rejoice with joy unspeakable and full of glory: Receiving the end of your faith, even the salvation of your souls." (I Peter 1:3-9)

Yes, when we walk with God, our future is bright. When Satan comes along with his devices to hurt and discourage us, when he tries to remind us of our past and present situation, we must just rebuke him and remind him of our future.

Let me give you these final thoughts to keep in mind when struggles come into your life. First of all, I challenge you to *Keep Godly Habits.* Pray continually when it is going good or bad, and read your Bible daily. "Thou wilt keep him in perfect peace, whose mind is stayed on thee: because he trusteth in thee." (Isaiah 26:3) Stop focusing on your problems, and stay focused on Christ.

Secondly, *Stay in Fellowship.* "Let *the* word of Christ dwell in you richly in all wisdom; teaching and admonishing one another in psalms and hymns and spiritual songs, singing with grace in your hearts to the Lord." (Colossians 3:16) Take time to focus on the need of others. Visit those who are sick in the hospital, and do not forget to be a mentor to a child. Stay close to your family members and let Christ always be in your conversation. In other words, do what you can do to create and keep an atmosphere that welcomes the presence of the Lord. When trouble comes (and it will come), you can rest in the fact that you have (for the most part) done all you can do. Now, the only thing you can do is stand and hold your hope. Hold your hope because the devil cannot win. He is already defeated. If he could have, he would have destroyed us by now, but we do not belong to him; we belong to God.

Thirdly, *Live Your Life One Day at a Time* and like Paul, be content with whatever your lot is for that day. A Senior Deacon shared this with me: "This is the day which the LORD hath made; we will rejoice and be glad in it."(Psalms 118:24)

Fourthly, *Do Not Give Up, and Do Not Give In.* As David did, sometimes you have to encourage yourself. Tell yourself, "I am a child of God, and I know God did not bring me this far to leave me". And, if you cannot do anything else, just Praise God. If you don't have any shoes, Praise Him that you have feet … no food, thank Him for water … no house, thank Him for your body clothed in your right mind. If you don't have anything, thank Him that you are saved.

Remember Job lost everything but his very life and soul. All he had to hold on to was hope, but that was a plenty. Look at what he lost, yet how all things were restored tremendously in the end. Hold your hope. Don't give up; don't give in; don't surrender; don't succumb … Hold your hope. God did not bring us safely this far to leave us … Hold your hope. "Weeping may endure for a night but joy comes in the morning." Hold your hope. Do not focus on your problem; rather, stay focused on Jesus Christ. You know they counted Him out one Friday Night, and in His darkest hour there on the cross, He, too, thought that God had forsaken Him; however, early Sunday Morning He had a new outlook on the situation. He had all power in His hand. Now, that power is available to us if we only Hold our Hope.

I leave you with these words on dealing with our struggles: Never get so low in your life that you dare think that you cannot reach up for the hand of God. Never get so high in your life that you dare not reach down to help others who are in need. Struggles come and go; they can hinder us or help us. The bottom line is that struggles are only tests to give us testimonies of how great God is and how life is truly abundant when we walk with Him. It is our challenge to make struggles stepping stones, not obstacles.

Step VI:
Having A Passion For Life

What is Life? "Whereas ye know not what shall be on the morrow. For what is your life?" Then this question is immediately answered: "It is even a vapour, that appeareth for a little time, and then vanisheth away." (James 4:14) A few days ago, I was listening to a televangelist as she described just how insignificant we are. She began by talking about how God is an Awesome God to create such a world, but not only the world, but also the Milky Way. To create our Solar System, filled with black holes and all kinds of galaxies and planets—just think of the God who made all of this. Really, when you think of the Universe, the earth becomes just a speck on the canvas of God's creation.

Now, if you can picture in your mind just how small the earth is compared to all the planets, solar systems, and galaxies around it, just think about man on the earth. When we look at the whole picture, we must admit that we are as the Bible has described; just a vapor. And, if we will be honest with ourselves, the only thing that makes this vapor important is the fact that God cares for us. The Bible calls us a vapour. "*It is a vapour that appeareth for a little time, and then vanisheth away*". "O, remember that my life is wind: mine eye shall no more see good."(Job 7:7) "For all flesh is as grass, and all the glory of man as the flower of grass. The grass withereth, and the flower thereof falleth away." (1 Peter 1:24) "But the rich, in that he is made low: because as the flower of the grass he shall pass away." (James 1:10)

The first thing we observe about life is that for whatever it is, life is short. The scripture bears this out again: "Man that is born of a woman is of few days, and full of trouble." (Job 14:1) In fact, life is too short—too short for us to be angry, bitter, upset, vengeful, grudge bearing, hateful, deceitful, or out of control with one another. That is one of my daily requests of the Lord: "Lord, let me follow peace with my fellow man."

As an example, let me give you a secret to a happy marriage. Judy and I have decided that we will not allow circumstances and situations to come between our relationship. We work at that; we pray about that, and we have some key words for each other. Her word for me is Carey and my word for her is Fru ... When we say those words a certain way, it sends a signal for us to settle down. We realize that as long as we feel good about each other, everything else will work itself out in a due process of time.

Life is too short. We must make every day special, every day count for good. Every day I want to celebrate life, want to enjoy it and make some sense of it. Celebrate life. Relax. Try not to ever be in a hurry for anything. Take deep breaths. Smell the flowers. Learn how to smile. Forgive people and forgive yourself. Celebrate life and make it last forever!!! Now, the obvious question is how can I make this short life a celebration that lasts forever? In other words, how can I have life, have it abundantly and everlastingly? How can I, even when I leave this world, even when I die, exist and be a celebration? Well, I want to suggest that we have worth, value, and can be sustained only when God looks upon us with favor. You know what? God does look upon us with favor. As a matter of fact, we are His crowned creation. Listen to the words of David:

> "O, LORD our Lord, how excellent is thy name in all the earth! who hast set thy glory above the heavens. Out of the mouth of babes and sucklings hast thou ordained strength because of thine enemies, that thou mightest still the enemy and the avenger. When I consider thy heavens, the work of thy fingers, the moon and the stars, which thou hast ordained; what is man, that thou art mindful of him? and the son of man, that thou visitest him? For thou hast made him a little lower than the angels, and hast crowned him with glory and honour. Thou madest him to have dominion over the works of thy hands; thou hast put all things under his feet: All sheep and oxen, yea, and the beasts of the field; the fowl of the air, and the fish of the sea, and whatsoever passeth through the paths of the seas. O, LORD our Lord, how excellent is thy name in all the earth!" (Psalms 8:1-9)

Furthermore, God cares so much for us that He planned a way to save us before He created us: "Then shall the King say unto them on his right hand, Come, ye blessed of my Father, inherit the kingdom prepared for you from the foundation of the world." (Matthew 25:34) "According as he hath chosen us in him before the foundation of the world, that we should be holy and without blame before him in love."(Ephesians 1:4) "And all that dwell upon the earth shall worship him, whose names are not written in the book of life of the Lamb slain from the foundation of the world." (Revelations 13:8)

How does He save us and give life everlasting? The answer is found in one of my favorite scriptures: "For God so loved the world, that he gave his only begotten Son, that whosoever believeth in him should not perish, but have everlasting life." (John 3:16) You hear and see that the only condition that God requires of us is that we believe. We must believe that God is who He says He is and that He can do what He says He can do ... through Jesus Christ. Everything else then is just the walk of life and it is as different as each individual. It is as unique as we all are.

Therefore, this leads me to another point that I want to make about what life is. Ultimately, we have no control over its future and the scripture infers that it is very foolish to think that we have. That is right. You and I do not know what is going to happen from one minute to the next. For all I know, I may be writing my last book. For all you know, you may be reading your last book. Who knows in this time of wars and rumors of war what will be our lot this time in another day, week, or month.

Life can be friendly; then life can be so unfair. I often view life as an adventure because every day is a challenge because you do not know what is going to happen next. But, whatever happens, you have to deal with it.

Some people jog, exercise, eat properly and get plenty of rest. Yet, they are sometimes stricken with some terrible disease and die early in adulthood. That's life. Paul told Timothy: "For bodily exercise profiteth little: but godliness is profitable unto all things, having promise of the life that now is, and of that which is to come."(1 Timothy 4:8) Then another may smoke, drink, curse and fuss and have bad eating habits; yet he may live to be 80 or 90 years old. That's life.

The whole fourth chapter of James is to remind us that we have absolutely no control over our future except to put our lives in the hand of God. You read it and you are challenged to stop fussing and feuding and making claims of what you are going to do, because nothing in life is a surety but God. This is stated specifically in the Book of James:

> "Go to now, ye that say, Today or tomorrow we will go into such a city, and continue there a year, and buy and sell, and get gain: Whereas ye know not what shall be on the morrow. For what is your life? It is even a vapour that appeareth for a little time, and then vanisheth away. For that ye ought to say, If the Lord will, we shall live, and do this, or that. But now ye rejoice in your boastings: all such rejoicing is evil. Therefore to him that knoweth to do good, and doeth it not, to him it is sin." (James 4:13-17)

John says it like this: "And the world passeth away, and the lust thereof: but he that doeth the will of God abideth for ever ..." (1 John 2:17)

Yes, life is short and we must learn to guard it. We must take full advantage of every day that we are blessed to walk on planet Earth. We must guard our life because carried in it is a very precious cargo. In other words, we must be sure to take care of our souls. That is the only sure thing that we have that never leaves us so we must keep it in good shape with God because it will always be with us. As a matter of fact, that is who we are. Our body is just a shell that shelters who we really are. The body reflects through smiles or frowns the love or hate of what we really are in our soul. Our only hope is in the resurrected Jesus. Paul makes this clear: "For in him we live, and move, and have our being; as certain also of your own poets have said, For we are also his offspring." (Acts 17:28) Compare Him, analyze Him, stand Christ beside any other god or religion and you will see that it just makes sense to follow Jesus. How then do we keep our soul sensitive to the will of God? How do we live in a chaotic world?

KEEP THAT PASSION FOR LIFE

One of my favorite scriptures in the Bible is: "I can do all things through Christ who strengthens me." (Philippians 4: 13) I thank my God daily for my life, for whatever I am going through, whether good or full of adversity, I see my life as an adventure. My confidence is that each day God will be standing with me.

I have seen on the news an Afghan woman being interviewed about the impending war that could come to that country. She said she did not care because life was not worth living anyway.

During a recent Christmas season, I went shopping at the mall and saw an old friend who was working in one of the stores. After I had bought a gift and exchanged greetings with him, I invited him to come to church and fellowship with us. He replied, "I won't promise you because I really don't see the point." When I asked him why he felt that way his reply was, "I really don't see the point of life. It simply doesn't make sense to me." Stunned by what he said, I walked away feeling somehow that I had failed him because I was leaving a man whose life was apparently so empty that he, in his own words, "don't see the point." I think how terrible, how horrible it must be to live in this world with no zeal for life, no sense of purpose, no direction, only emptiness, and unhappiness.

Unfortunately, I am beginning to see that a lot of people go through this adventure I call life only existing, but not living life as God intended. Let me ask you: What is your purpose for being here? What if I told you God had a purpose, a definite plan for all of us? What is your ministry? What are your short and your long-range goals? If you cannot answer questions like these, could it be that you are not living you life to it fullest potential? Are you just existing, reacting to others and the things around you? I am sure you will agree with me that for whatever life is, it is too short not to enjoy it; it is too short not to appreciate it, and it is too short not to have meaning to it. I am so saddened by the fact that too many people exist but do not live. Too many people are depressed and oppressed. They view life as one big cycle of pain, hurt, and trouble. They see no way out and therefore they see themselves as failures. Some even feel doomed. Satan wants us living a defeated and doomed life. Observe the words of John: "The thief cometh not, but for to steal, and to kill, and to destroy: I am come that they might have life, and that they might have it more abundantly." (John 10:10)

With that in mind, I want to extend my definition of life. Life might also be defined as the quality manifested in functions such as metabolism, growth, response to stimulation, and reproduction by which living organisms are distinguished from the dead. It is the physical and emotional covering of the soul that when stimulated by God does good and sometimes mighty acts and deeds over and over again. However, the problem is that Satan is a thief; he is a taker of life. He comes to steal, kill, and destroy your life. His desire is to stunt your growth, steal your joy, kill your spirit, and literally destroy your life. If he had his way, all of us would be dead right now—spiritually, emotionally, and physically. This is Satan's ultimate objective and he has some of us two-thirds of the way there having already destroyed some people spiritually and emotionally. They are alive, but are like walking zombies without existence except to do his will. Satan is a taker; he uses drugs and alcohol and has promiscuous sex to sap our physical strength and emotional will. He grasps our peace and uses up all our physical energy and material resources. In other words, he keeps us tired and broke. That is why I tell people all the time that we should not work on a job we do not enjoy. That is just too much time and energy spent and not enough money made to work a job we are not happy with. The same might be true in any relationship where we are not fulfilled and happy. Again, Satan is a thief and he wants our life.

On the other hand, Jesus says, "I am come that they might have life, and that they might have it more abundantly." Now I want to remind you again and again that the only way you can experience life is to let Christ be your Lord and Savior. It is not magical, and it does not change things over night, but He can make a difference. He can turn your life around. It is my belief that Jesus is the answer. Jesus is the reason for the seasons, and it is Jesus who gives us abundant life. Therefore, the point I make about life is this: Every day set before you is life and death, blessings and curses. Everyday you have a choice to make—a choice to live for Jesus or to live for Satan. You are going to experience life abundantly, or you have a choice to experience life as a living hell.

Every day there are the choices we have, and every day these are the choices we make. Regardless of the situation and circumstances, every day we all have to go through something. Life is not easy. God never said it would be. Tell me a story about your life, and I can tell you a story about mine. We all have our troubles, but when you walk through life with Jesus, he will give you comfort in times of trouble. He will give you joy in times of sorrow. He will make you strong in your weakness. He will bring peace in the midst of your confusion. That is why you never call a day bad until you have gone through the whole day.

Jesus said: "These things I have spoken unto you, that in me ye might have peace. In the world ye shall have tribulation: but be of good cheer; I have overcome the world."(John 16:33) Jesus overcame the world when He was resurrected from the grave, and since He has overcome the world, remember that if your problem is not greater than the resurrection, then you do not have a problem at all. Thank God, you are never alone. Our challenge is to simply make the right choices everyday. The problem is we oftentimes choose not to follow Christ and become failures. Then, some people remain failures all of their lives.

Let me shock you all with this statement: We all are or have been failures most of our lives. Yes, we all are kin to failure. I know someone is thinking, "Oh no, I am not a failure, never been a failure." Well, that is part of your problem. You will not face the truth about yourself. We all have miserably failed in life most of the time where it really mattered. Let me show you: "For all have sinned, and come short of the glory of God." (Romans 3:23) Remember, in your unsaved life, all those ugly, hurtful, foolish, harmful things you did? The old saints said it like this, "I wasn't fit to live, but not ready to die." What they were saying was: they were failures. Don't you know you can be a success in this world, the world of entrepreneurs, entertainment and society, yet still be a failure? "For what shall it profit a man, if he shall gain the whole world, and lose his own soul?" (Mark 8:36) Remember the story of Ebenezer Scrooge. Scrooge had money, power, and the potential to have most everything the world could offer, yet he did not have anything because he did not really have a life. He merely existed. His attitude was negative. He showed no compassion for others and his passion for life was misguided. Just in time, the Spirit of Christmas redirected him. That is a great story. This was our plight until we found meaning to life in a relationship with Christ.

Even now as a saved child of God, can you say that you are absolutely and completely in the will of God, and doing the will of God? I do not know about you, but I am glad that God's Grace is sufficient because even now I confess I fail the Lord in so many ways.

My point is that just because we were once failures, and even fail at some things now, it does not mean we have to live as failures. We cannot allow our failures to get the best of us. We cannot wallow in our letdowns, nor throw ourselves a pity party. If we choose wisely, there can be life after failure. Yes, there is life after jail, life after sickness, life after bankruptcy, life after feuds, life after mistakes, life after trouble, and if you live right, there is life after death. To avoid getting stuck in our failures, we must let them go. I don't know about you, but I do not choose to remain focused on my past failures. Some of us need to pray and ask God to make some adjustments in our attitudes to remind us that we are His children.

Listen, we are the King's Kid. That is my attitude and I am not bragging. I am praising God because I belong to Him and that is so important. Listen to this scripture: "For where your treasure is, there will your heart be also."(Luke 12:34) Daily, I am determined to make my treasures consist with the things of God. This idea ensures the welfare of my heart. Furthermore, we must guard our feelings and keep our emotions in check. Take, for example, the tragedy of September11, 2001. I had prayed, watched, and tried to help. Then the time came when I had to distance myself from so much news about that because I refused to keep absorbing that down in my spirit. You have to watch what you allow to absorb in your spirit. If you are going to live life and live it abundantly, shed that fear of failure mentality.

How do you do that? Admit it and move on. Satan can never hurt me with my failures if I admit them and move on. When I confess my fears, faults, and failures to God, I move on. Consequently, when Satan brings them up, I rebuke him because I have already confessed them to God and moved on. I refuse to let Satan bring up my confessed past. Why should I be concerned with what God has already forgiven me? Yes, I am a failure but I am moving on. By the way, do not ever forget that God uses failures. Noah was a righteous man; yet, he had a drinking problem. Abraham, Father of our Faith, sometimes told lies. Jacob, whose name was changed to Israel, gave birth to the Nation of God; yet, he was the greatest of deceivers and tricksters in the Bible. Rahab, the grandmother of David, the great-great grandmother of Solomon, and the great grandmother of Jesus, had been a prostitute.

My point is that great ministries are born from pain and shame. All we need to do is to turn our lives over to the Good Shepherd. He can turn our failure into victory. Only God can give us a sense of self, who we are, why we are here, and where we are going. Only the Good Shepherd can "create in us a clean heart and renew within us the right spirit." Only the Good Shepherd can give us the attitude adjustment we need so that we can say, "I am somebody" and have that right feeling to say like old James Brown, "Oh, I feel good."

Some people, However allow their fears, faults, and failures to keep them from the abundant life that the Good Shepherd has promised. Some people let old age, sickness, or financial problems keep them in a world of despair, but I do not choose to be that way. When I think about the fact that I am a King's Kid, it ignites a fire and a passion in me. God is with me. Do you know how precious it is for God to be with us? Do you believe that? I do. God came into the world some 2000 years ago and one name given him was Emmanuel, which means, "God is with Us." Yes, I know God is with me, and that makes me special. That means if I choose to, I can be the head and not the tail. I cannot only be a follower, but I can also be a leader. Why? Because I know, who I am and whose I am. I am a child of God. Therefore, I am a joint heir with Christ. I am his little brother; I have been saved into royalty. That means, "I can do all things through Christ who strengthens me." I have people all around me who bear witness that you can have life and have it more abundantly.

> "Wherefore seeing we also are compassed about with so great a cloud of witnesses, let us lay aside every weight, and the sin which doth so easily beset us, and let us run with patience the race that is set before us, Looking unto Jesus the author and finisher of our faith; who for the joy that was set before him endured the cross, despising the shame, and is set down at the right hand of the throne of God." (Hebrews 12: 1-2)

Finally, I want to share some things that have helped me to have a passion for life.

1. Live one day at a time.

Living one day at a time is all you can live anyway. I received an email about the bombing of the Twin Towers relating it to the prophecy of Nostradamus. I clicked delete so fast because I do not have time to worry about the future like that. It is stated in the book of Matthew: "Take therefore no thought for the morrow: for the morrow shall take thought for the things of itself. Sufficient unto the day is the evil thereof." (Matthew 6:34) Make today a great day. Make every day special; make every day count. What a privilege it is to be alive today. And, we ought to live today as if it were our last because we do not ever know.

2. Love.

You can have passion and a joy for life if you love. God is love, not hate, not envy, not bitterness. God always gives me the upper hand in life because I have learned to love people unconditionally. Love always finds a way.

> "Charity suffereth long, and is kind; charity envieth not; charity vaunteth not itself, is not puffed up, Doth not behave itself unseemly, seeketh not her own, is not easily provoked, thinketh no evil; Rejoiceth not in iniquity, but rejoiceth in the truth; Beareth all things, believeth all things, hopeth all things, endureth all things. Charity never faileth ..." (1 Corinthians 13:4-8)

It is hard for the world and folk to bother you when you have the love of God in your heart.

3. Pray and Meditate.

This is your source of power. Get up in the morning with prayer and meditation and God will lead your life. Proverbs states: "In all thy ways acknowledge him, and he shall direct thy paths." (Proverbs 3: 6) If you talk with God, then you can walk with God.

4. Serve Others.

Happiness comes in serving others. Helping, sharing, and caring will cause God and his people to set you in a special place. God showers us with unforeseen blessings if we serve others. Use your gifts to share with others and He will share more gifts with you. Remember the story of the talents. When stewards used the ones they had, God doubled them. The more you give, the more you shall receive.

5. Don't worry.

Karl Barth says, "Courage is fear that has said its prayers." Work through your worries with prayers.

6. Smile.

It takes fewer muscles to smile than to frown. A smile is universal. A smile means that you are happy with who you are and with the world around you. Carey Ingram says, "A smile is the soul on the inside smiling on the outside. Smile wards off negativity."

7. Don't be negative, and stay away from negative folk.

Do not listen to folk who are always talking other people down. Don't you know they are saying the same things about you when you are not around? The Bible says that people curse you by the things they say, so, don't be where you absorb that stuff in your spirit. Do not listen to folk who tell you that you can't do something. That is how folk keep you back. You have to follow your dreams and follow the path of the Lord. If you fail, turn your failure into stepping-stones in order to move up. I heard someone say that failure is like a fire refinery. God is molding and working with us. As the song says, "Please be patient with me; God is not through with me yet. But when God gets through with me, I shall come forth as pure gold."

Look at the word "life." Take the "f" out of life and it becomes the word "lie." I want to suggest that in my explanation "F" stands for God the Father. It comes to mind that if you take the letter "f" out of the word life, your life becomes a lie. It becomes something false and slanted. Your life without the Father is something He did not intend for you to be. Let it be our purpose to keep the Father in our life so that we might have an abundant and passionate life that will take us where we never dreamed we could go.

Step VII:
Suffering Is Redemptive

One of my first encounters with pain was a fateful day when my grandmother, a hair dresser, told me, "Son, don't touch that hotplate." I don't remember exactly how old I was, around five or six, but I do remember the incident and the pain. Isn't it something that those things that hurt us, cause us pain, and cause us to suffer are the ones we remember. As I write this, I am referring to an incident that happened some 45 years ago, yet I can see it as if it happened yesterday. Why? I remember the pain and the suffering.

My grandmother was what we then called a "beauticianist". She had her beauty salon in the basement of our home and one Saturday as she was leaving the shop to go to someone's home to do their hair, she came out with some curling irons and a little hot plate that had a kind of metal covering over it. I was outside riding my bike. She said to me, "Son, don't touch this hotplate." I said, "Yes ma'm, Grandma." But, it was like her telling me, "Carey, please just as soon as I leave, go and touch that hot plate for something awaits you if you do." Just as soon as she was out of sight, I got off my bike and it was like I was compelled to touch that hot plate. You know, your parents tell you not to do something, but you do it just to see what happens.

It is apparent that at the time, I did not know just how hot and cold worked. I walked over to that hot plate and what did I do? I laid the palm of my hand down on the covering of that hot plate and burned myself. I do not believe I have ever experienced such physical pain as that since. It was the kind of pain when a child begins to cry, he cries so hard and with so much determination that the cry is silent and he come close to losing his breath. It was that kind of cry because it was that kind of pain. Not only that, but I remember the days that followed and that my hand was swollen and blistered. In those days, parents would put butter on a burned injury. However, only slow time healed my wound. I do not remember the pain of my illness when I was in the hospital at the age of four, but the hotplate incident was my first recollection of pain and suffering.

What is suffering? What is pain? The Merriam-Webster dictionary defines suffering as "to submit to or be forced to endure some degree of pain and/or distress." Suffering may also mean experiencing a sustained loss or damage, subject to disability. It can be physical as caused by an injury or disease. Suffering may be emotional pain caused by grief from a death, mental abuse, or acute mental distress.

The obvious question that arises is: Why do we suffer or why is there suffering in the world especially when you are trying to live above it? You are living with the belief that you are God's child. You minister to others; you help those who are in need and those who are less fortunate than yourself. You go out of your way to share with others the "Good News" of Jesus. Yet, sometimes life's response to your good deeds seems to be trials, tribulations, and persecutions. You can only wonder, WHY? WHY? WHY, LORD, IS ALL THIS HAPPENING TO ME? Whereas I do not know all the answers about suffering, one thing is for sure: suffering is inevitable and it is going to happen. Listen to what the Bible says about suffering: "Man that is born of a woman is of few days, and full of trouble. He cometh forth like a flower, and is cut down: he fleeth also as a shadow, and continueth not."(Job 14:1-2) "These things I have spoken unto you, that in me ye might have peace. In the world ye shall have tribulation: but be of good cheer; I have overcome the world." (John 16:33)

It is Paul's trial of the thorn in his flesh that helps me to understand why we must suffer. Observe the scripture that helps us to know that suffering can be an ally for us:

> "And lest I should be exalted above measure through the abundance of the revelations, there was given to me a thorn in the flesh, the messenger of Satan to buffet me, lest I should be exalted above measure. For this thing I besought the Lord thrice, that it might depart from me. And he said unto me, My grace is sufficient for thee: for my strength is made perfect in weakness. Most gladly therefore will I rather glory in my infirmities, that the power of Christ may rest upon me. Therefore I take pleasure in infirmities, in reproaches, in necessities, in persecutions, in distresses for Christ's sake: for when I am weak, then am I strong." (II Corinthians 12:7-10)

In a vision the Apostle had been taken to a level of Heaven. By now he had experienced a spiritual awareness and a power of Christ not known to many at that time. God had given Paul deep and intimate spiritual experiences. In other words, Paul was a servant of God with power, and he knew this. Because of this,

God Himself had given Paul a "thorn in the flesh" as a way of keeping him close to Him. Three significant points can be made from these scriptures.

First, there was a need for a "thorn" in the flesh to keep Paul in the right relationship with God. It was for Paul and is also imperative for us to know that despite our relationship with God, we are no better than others. We, like Paul, are always totally dependent upon God despite our spiritual experiences. What was the "thorn in the flesh?" There are many suggestions as to what it was. Some spiritual suffering comes in the form of constant attacks by Satan, opposition by men, or occasional evangelistic failure to keep Paul humble and on his face before God seeking guidance and strength. There is also some physical suffering such as a recurring fever, malaria, epilepsy, or poor eyesight.

Just what the thorn was is not specifically identified. My belief is some physical ailment for suffering is what this passage is all about.(See II Corinthians 11:16; 12:10.) The words flesh, strength, weakness, and infirmities are used, and although these same words could be used to describe spiritual sufferings, the context does not weigh toward spiritual suffering. (II Corinthians 10:10) The clearest description of the thorn is probably eye trouble. (Acts 9:8-9); II Corinthian 10:10; and Galatians 4:13-15; 6:11) Paul had been stricken blind for three days and stoned several times. (II Corinthian 11:24-27). A serious injury to his eyes, or for that matter to any other part of his body, could have occurred at any of these tragedies.

Second, Paul wanted relief from his pain and suffering because it seemed to make him weak and sickly. But most of all, it kept him from doing his best for the Kingdom of God. Paul wanted relief; he prayed and yet what was given to him was not the relief he asked for. God refused to remove the thorn from Paul's flesh for two reasons:

1. The thorn served to keep Paul from being exalted above measure. In other words, the thorn in his flesh kept him humble.

2. God wanted to reveal His power to Paul. The weaker the vessel, the more God is glorified when the vessel really serves God.

God's answer to Paul's prayer was: "My grace is sufficient for thee." The presence, love, favor, and blessings of God are sufficient to help your walk through any suffering. The word "sufficient" means the power or strength to withstand any danger. God's grace within can carry you through anything. In Paul's case, it was physical suffering.

God stated: "My strength is made perfect in weakness." (II Corinthian 12:9) The weaker the believer, the more God can demonstrate His strength. If you are self-sufficient, you do not need God; but, if you are weak, you need the help, provision, and sufficiency of God. He further states: "Most gladly, therefore, will I rather glory in my infirmities that the power of Christ may rest upon me." (II Corinthian 12:9) The point here is infirmities or weaknesses are purposeful. You suffer so that the power of Christ may be demonstrated and clearly seen in your life. The idea is that the power of Christ rests upon the suffering believer just as the Shekinah glory dwelt in the holy place of the tabernacle. What a glorious thought. The strength of Christ fixes itself upon you and dwells within you-filling you with the Shekinah glory of God when you suffer.

The third and final reason God would not remove the thorn is because He wanted Paul to live "for Christ's sake." Remember, our infirmities give Christ an opportunity to prove who He is, and what He can do. Therefore, we are to do what Paul did: take pleasure in infirmities and all kinds of sufferings and weaknesses, whether emotional or physical. Take pleasure in reproaches whether they are ridicule, insult, slander, or rumor. Take pleasure in necessities which could be hardships, need, deprivation, hunger, thirst, lack of shelter or clothing, or any other necessity. Take pleasure in persecutions that come in the form of verbal or physical attacks, abuse, or injury. Take pleasure in distresses, those tight situations, perplexities, disturbances, anxious moments, depressions, inescapable problems and difficulties. If you can take pleasure in these things, you will find that when you are weak, you are actually strong. How? By the power of Christ which is much stronger than all the combined forces of sin, evil, and mankind.

I must confess to you that taking pleasure in your suffering is easier said than done. The truth is, in recent months, I have had such an experience. When I first began to write on the subject of "Steps Toward Abundant Living", I had no idea as to the things that God would allow me to go through in order to complete this very important work. I will explain in detail what my sufferings were later. However, I am here to tell you that it was the suffering, the physical pain and the mental anguish that has brought about such a great change. It is like I was born again. God, indeed, has moved me to another level. I once heard a man say that you can always tell when God is working the worst things out for your good because when He is done with you, you are not bitter, you are better. And that is so true in my life. Romans 8:28 has been a favorite verse of mine for as long as I can remember: "And we know that all things work together for good to them that love God, to them who are the called according to his purpose." Daily, I have had to stand on that verse. It seems as if I could not even feel the presence of God, but

I just kept praying, hoping, believing, reading and meditating until one day just as suddenly as my trials and tribulations had come, they were gone. "To God be the Glory." That was my life at 49, but trials and tribulations can and will come at any time. The point is that we simply have to learn to trust God with our life. We must learn to use suffering as an ally. Paul said to learn to be content.

In his sermon, Pastor Robert E. Houston, Sr. of Nashville, Tennessee made some key points concerning this scripture: "Not that I speak in respect of want: for I have learned, in whatsoever state I am, therewith to be content." (Philippians 4: 11). Here are the key points made in this excerpt from his sermon: There is a song written by Brewster Highley entitled, "Home, Home on the Range." The lyrics go something like this:

> "Oh, give me a home where the buffalo roam
> Where the deer and the antelope play
> Where seldom is heard a discouraging word
> And the skies are not cloudy all day."

The inference of this song suggests that the writer of the song is contemplating life itself and he is suggesting that life is better when we are away from the trappings of our daily lives. This writer says that it can be discouraging being around the job, home, friends, family, grocery stores, churches, beauty shops, barber shops, restaurants, banks, television, movies, and taking time for exercising and dieting ever day. This writer says that if he had a choice, he would trade it all in and pack up and go outside—relocate to the country and the wilderness. He says the reason for his relocation is because he cannot find many discouraging words among the animals and plants. Further, he says that the skies look better. The circumstances over his head look better away from where he is.

The truth of the matter is that discouraging words and cloudy skies may affect some folk, but the child of God who knows that the Lord is his light and his salvation also knows that "weeping may endure for a night but joy cometh in the morning." The child of God who recognizes that no weapon formed against him shall prosper will not allow that which is around him to speak to him. He has a higher level; he has a higher understanding; he has a higher listening gauge. In other words, a child of God is able to RISE ABOVE the pressures, trials and tests of this world and learns to be content.

From my standpoint, I am not going to allow the Devil or any demons to dictate to me my contentment. War in Iraq—I am still content. Gay marriage in San Francisco—I am still content. Politics going on—I am still content. Trouble in the streets—I am still content. Gas prices skyrocketing a gallon—I am still content. Having to watch my back at all times—I am still content. Facing surgery—I am still content. Enemies all around me—I am still content.

My contentment is not based on my circumstances. I am looking at some folk right now whose circumstances could make you go crazy if you let them, but our circumstances do not make you more content or less content. You can own a projection TV and still be miserable. You can own a $400,000 home and still be miserable. You can have his and her Cadillacs and still be miserable. You can make $150,000 a year and still be miserable. You can have a swimming pool and a Jacuzzi in the backyard and still be miserable. You can wear $500 glasses and $500 shoes and have $500 in your pocket and still be miserable.

The Apostle Paul deals with this in his letter to the Philippian church. The context is that Paul had been under arrest and in a Roman jail system. He had been assisted by the Philippians time and time again because even though they were poor in finance, they were big in heart. Paul opens his letter up by saying, "I am not writing because I am seeking more money from you. I am not writing because of what I want. My wants are not at issue here." Here are three major points to keep in your spirit:

I. LIFE HAS TAUGHT ME SOMETHING.

First of all, I do not speak in regards to what I want because I have seen what God has done in the past. Second, God used you to take care of me, but ultimately it was God who blessed me. You see in the past; I have learned that God was the one who took care of me. Let me suggest that you may have a job, but you got it from Jesus. You may have a house, but you got it from Jesus. You may have gotten a welfare check from the State of California, but it came from Jesus. Third, do not forget that God has given us something wonderful. He gives us memory, and memory is the replay button of the soul. When trouble comes, we walk around burdened and sorrowful rather than hit the replay button and say, "He brought me through before and he gave me victory before. He healed me." Fourth, Paul does not express his wants to the Philippian Church because he understood that whatever you want, asking people for it will get you strange results. Rather, whatever you need, ask God for it. If you ask him in secret, he will reward you openly.

II. LIFE DOES CHANGE.

Your life can change at the blink of an eye. All it takes is a phone call, a letter, or a confrontation. All it takes is a hospital visit or a surgical procedure. Life does change. The reason why some people are not content is that they do not understand that God is orchestrating what they are going through. Rather than to rejoice in their circumstances and to have peace, they would rather sulk and pout, rather than to be content. The Devil will try to tell you to give up in your pain. The Devil will try to tell you that you are not going to make it. But listen, when life changes, tell God "Thank you." When life changes, thank Him for what He is trying to teach us. If a change happens in your life, thank God for it and be content. If someone leaves you, thank God and be content. If you lose your job, thank God and be content. If trouble comes to your house, thank God and be content.

Why should we be content? Well, my experiences teach me some things. First, I have to understand that I am not the first one to go through some things. And then secondly, I am not the only one going through some things. And then lastly, I will not be the last one to go through some things. However, I equally have to say that I am not going through this situation by myself. God promises that he is with me. In Bible Study we learned that God is with us. In the Old Testament, God was with us. In the New Testament, Jesus was with us in flesh. In the New Testament and now, we have the Holy Spirit with us and in us. So, whenever I go through something, I am not alone; He is with me. So, it is not that I am going through; it is *we* are going through. So, it is not I am having trouble; it is *we* are having trouble. And I know that God will not leave nor forsake us.

III. I WILL BE CONTENT.

Paul says that when I look at my circumstances now, I have learned that whatever my lot in life to be content. First, he defines contentment. Consider this: The word content is [autarkes/ow·tar·kace/]. Autarkes means three things: 1. Sufficient for one's self, strong enough or processing enough to need no aid or support; 2. Independent of external circumstances; 3. Contented with one's lot, with one's means, though the slenderest. It seems to suggest that my contentment is not made by external circumstances. It suggests that I am satisfied even though I do not have all I want but I do have what I need.

I have Jesus. The tougher things get, the more I find out who Jesus really is. I find out He is a Way-maker. Some things I thought I would never escape, but I found out Jesus is a deliverer. Some things I thought I would never get healed from, but God is a heart fixer and a mind regulator.

May I suggest that even though your times and your circumstances may get lean, you do have what you need. May I suggest that even though trouble comes, you do have what you need.

> I can be content even though trouble rises.
> I can be content even though storm comes.
> I can be content even though sickness comes.

Because of Jesus, I will not only survive, but I will thrive even through my suffering and pain.

Step VIII:
Three Essentials To Happiness

Like many people, one of our family vacation spots is Orlando, Florida. It is the home of the Mickey Mouse of Disney Land and about 10 others major theme parks. When our children were in their early teens, we would get up early and stay all day and night at these fun parks. Believe it or not, we thought it was fun standing in 45 minute lines for 5 minute rides. We enjoyed the food, people, and the fun atmosphere. It has been only in recent years that we have gone to Florida and found fun in just resting around our villa. That might entail a round of golf, a short walk, or just relaxing around the pool with a book.

It was on an occasion of just relaxing on our patio that I formulated in my mind what it really means to be happy. On this particular morning, my wife, Judy, sat beside me with a devotional book in her hand. She got up for a moment and playfully laid her book on my head. I opened this book up to these words by a man named Joseph Addison. Mr. Addison says, "There are three essentials to happiness … there must be something to do, someone to love, and something to hope for."

Now, not like many of my vacations, I had brought no laptop or books of my own. I had made no plans to work on any sermons or do anything that suggested any type of work which would require me to do any serious thinking. Rather, it was simply the words of this man that had a profound effect on me. It set my mind in motion. What does it really mean to be happy?

We find this definition in the words of Jesus in the "Sermon On The Mount". I am referring here to "The Beatitudes." Jesus began His sermon with the Beatitudes, starting with "Blessed are." When you read the Beatitudes, you can substitute the word happy in place of blessed. Happy are the poor in spirit: for theirs is the kingdom of heaven. Happy are they that mourn: for they shall be comforted. Happy are the meek: for they shall inherit the earth. Happy are they which do hunger and thirst after righteousness: for they shall be filled. Happy are the merciful: for they shall obtain mercy. Happy are the pure in heart: for they shall see God. Happy are the peacemakers: for they shall be called the children of God.

Happy are they which are persecuted for righteousness sake: for theirs is the kingdom of heaven. Happy are ye, when men shall revile you, and persecute you, and shall say all manner of evil against you falsely, for my sake. Rejoice, and be exceeding glad: for great is your reward in heaven: for so persecuted they the prophets which were before you. (Matthew 5:1-12)

For me, Jesus has given a litany of the trials and tribulations of life. The good part is that behind each of these heartaches and hardships is a great reward on earth and in heaven. Remember this: When you invest your life in Christ, there are always rewards. You cannot lose with Christ. You can only win. At the end of the day, week, month, year, and of your life, you are blessed.

Everyone wants to be blessed. Life is too short not to be happy but happiness is not obtained by accident. It is not something we stumble across. It is something we plan. There is a saying, "If you fail to plan, then you plan to fail." Happiness then can be obtained when we pursue this adventure we call life with Christ as our guide. Christ said this specifically in Matthew: "But seek ye first the kingdom of God, and his righteousness; and all these things shall be added unto you." (Matthew 6:33)

Therefore, we must seek happiness not through the temporal things of this world, but rather through the kingdom of God. I do not depend on anything or anybody for my happiness for it comes from within, and as a result, from my relationship with God through Jesus Christ. If I keep my relationship with Him solid, then my life is fulfilled and I am blessed and happy. I may lose some battles, but I know that I already have the victory and that alone gives me the peace of mind I need to press on.

Addison said that in order to be happy, you must "have something to do." James, the Apostle and half brother of Jesus, makes this declaration: "But be ye doers of the word, and not hearers only, deceiving your own selves. For if any be a hearer of the word, and not a doer, he is like unto a man beholding his natural face in a glass." (James 1:22-23)

My wife says that I am a hard sleeper and when I wake in the morning my hair is in disarray because of how I have tossed and turned. There is dry saliva around my mouth from my inability to keep my mouth closed while I sleep and my eyes are blood shot red. Now, what if when I arose, I looked into the mirror and saw how bad I looked, but then skipped all of my personal hygiene and grooming chores? What if I went straight to the closet and put on clean clothes but neglected my body? Not only would I look like a mad man, I probably would not last long on my job. Well, the word of God is like looking into a mirror and seeing all the wrong things in your life. Yet, James is inferring that too many times we see ourselves and do nothing to change those terrible things. In other words, there is no spiritual personal hygiene or grooming. If you are going to be happy, you must be a doer of the word. And the first thing you do is to apply the word to your own life. Think about this. How can you help others if your spiritual life is lacking? However, when our lives are in line with the word of God, and when we are doers of the word, we find happiness. Moreover, we are then qualified and capable of doing things that help others.

Happiness is having something to do. Now, that is not to say we are to be busybodies. My definition of a busybody is someone who does a lot of things all the time but the problem is it is not wholesome, positive, or productive in the eyes of God or in the lives of people. Believe me when I say that the world is full of busybodies who do the wrong things for the wrong reasons. Their motivation is generally selfish and self-centered. Busybodies *scatter people from* rather than *gather people to* the kingdom of God. If you are miserable, perhaps you are not doing something of real value. Remember the adage, "An idle mind is the devil's workshop." Remember, desire in your heart to do something of value and then act from your heart; do only those things which are good and positive.

The Psalmist says it best:

> "The steps of a good man are ordered by the LORD: and he delighteth in his way. Though he fall, he shall not be utterly cast down: for the LORD upholdeth him with his hand. I have been young, and now am old; yet have I not seen the righteous forsaken, nor his seed begging bread. He is ever merciful, and lendeth; and his seed is blessed. Depart from evil, and do good; and dwell for evermore." (Psalms 37:23-27)

Daily seek the Lord and then from the very depths of your soul, let Him lead you to do good deeds and watch your life blossom into something very rewarding and blessed. I am convinced that our greatest rewards are always found in helping someone else. It has been my joy for almost two decades to work with children in the summer time. The National Youth Sports Program (NYSP) is a program that provides a positive outlet for underprivileged children for six weeks on a college campus. It is challenging, but the rewards are tremendous. I watch some of these students graduate from our program and go on to be policemen, lawyers, and other productive citizens. All of us who work with these students have adopted a saying that has become a part of my philosophy of life: "I shall never pass this way but once. Any good that I can do, any kindness I can show, let me do it now for I shall never pass this way again."

The second essential to happiness is "having someone to love." Ancient Greeks give the world a definition of love in three degrees. There is "Eros" love for a man and woman only in order to consummate their relationship and have children. It is necessary to continue the evolution of human life and the most sensual way that a married couple demonstrates again and again their love. I fondly say that it is that "urge to merge" love. The second degree is "Phileos" love. This is "brotherly love" for neighbor, community, and country. It is a general love for life in which you reach out to those around you. It has been said that Philadelphia, Pennsylvania got its name from the Greeks. Phileo leads to Philadelphia, or "The City of Brotherly Love." The third degree is "Agape" love. This type comes from God. That is to say, you can only demonstrate this love when the spirit of God permeates your heart and moves you to do what you could not do otherwise. God's love is an unconditional love that asks for nothing in return in spite of what it might cost the one who demonstrates it. My personal definition of this love is "an infection from God that causes a unique affection for all of life around you." Yes, love from God is like a "holy germ" that infects the heart and spreads all over the body, soul, and mind. It changes you and in time you change the world around you. It is contagious and when close to others, this wonderful germ will infect them as well.

In the Bible, it is John, the beloved of Jesus, who gives us a very special understanding of love in relationship to God and our fellow man.

> "Beloved, let us love one another: for love is of God; and every one that loveth is born of God, and knoweth God. He that loveth not knoweth not God; for God is love. In this was manifested the love of God toward us, because that God sent his only begotten Son into the world, that we might live through him. Herein is love, not that we loved God, but that he loved us, and sent his Son to be the propitiation for our sins. Beloved, if God so loved us, we ought also to love one another. No man hath seen God at any time. If we love one another, God dwelleth in us, and his love is perfected in us." (I John 4:7-12)

Now, notice how John closes his chapter on love. "We love him, because he first loved us. If a man say, I love God, and hateth his brother, he is a liar: for he that loveth not his brother whom he hath seen, how can he love God whom he hath not seen? And this commandment have we from him, That he who loveth God loves his brother also."(1 John 4: 19-21)

No one can deny the power of love. When it is demonstrated, as the Bible suggests, we become powerful agents or ambassadors of God. We then are blessed and bless those around us. The question is: Do you possess that "agape" love? Well, take what I call "the love test." It is found in Matthew and it is Jesus who gives us this test and it is hard. Jesus said,

> "Ye have heard that it hath been said, Thou shalt love thy neighbour, and hate thine enemy. But I say unto you, Love your enemies, bless them that curse you, do good to them that hate you, and pray for them which despitefully use you, and persecute you; That ye may be the children of your Father which is in heaven: for he maketh his sun to rise on the evil and on the good, and sendeth rain on the just and on the unjust. For if ye love them which love you, what reward have ye? Do not even the publicans the same?" (Matthew 5: 43-46)

Love my enemies … WHAT? Bless them that curse me … Do good to them that hate you … COME ON! Pray for them who use me and persecute me. This is not fair; neither is it just, but it is God's way. It is God's love and it is what He requires of us if we are to be blessed and to make a difference in this world. Now, guess what I have discovered in this process? When you practice those responses toward your enemies, there is nothing else they can do to you. What a joy, what a peace I have when my enemies have done all they can do to me and I still care for them; yes, I mean genuinely love them. Rather than retaliate, you feel a sense of pity for your oppressor. You recognize their hurt that may not have anything to do with you personally. You want to help them rather than hurt them. You sense the power of God working in you to help, not hurt, to encourage but not cast down. God speaks to you and tells you to take the high road of His love and you find yourself standing above all the hate and bitterness of the situation. I tell you there is no greater victory than when you love those who come against you. In time you can win some people over to your way of thinking, but you must first pass the test.

There is a story that demonstrates this power of love. Brandi was seven years old when her mother died. She was an only child and her parents were poor. They were a Christian family and in spite of their tough life, they were happy. However, when her mother died, it seemed to take all of life from Brandi's dad, Charles. He was a good man, but he never stopped mourning the death of his wife and in the process started drinking and neglecting his daughter. It seemed now that alcohol was his life, and in time, was viewed as the town drunk. He lost his regular job, and had to resort to odd jobs. They made just enough money to pay the rent and to support his bad habit.

Brandi managed things the best she could. She was in school now and had to take care of herself. She would fix whatever food that was available at breakfast and at dinner times. She would dress and groom herself the best she could. Friends and neighbors would help her by sharing clothes, and dropping off food for her to eat, but it was a hard life. Finally, after a couple of year, the authorities came by and examined their home. They made it clear to Brandi that she did not have to stay in the home. They offered to place her in a foster home where she could have a better life. Brandi begged them not to take her away from her dad. She managed to convince them that she would be all right and that her dad would be OK only if she stayed with him. The authorities, sensing Brandi's love for her father, allowed her to stay in the home.

By the time she was ten years old, things were not any better and in fact, things had gotten worse. Often, the electricity or some other utility would be turned off. Brandi, upon hearing a siren from an ambulance or police car, would walk down the city streets in search of her dad, fearing something had happened to him. She would find him in saloons or on a corner often in a drunken state. She would literally walk, carry, and drag him home; often they would fall. She never complained even with tears in her eyes and her heart aching. She just did what she had to do. In this condition, Charles would often urinate on himself. She never let that bother her although it was embarrassing as neighbors looked from the windows and front doors to watch Brandi's struggle. She knew her dad was living with a broken heart that never seemed to mend. It was as though Brandi was the parent and Charles was the child. She did all she could to love him in spite of his problems.

One morning after Charles had been drinking all night, he woke as usual to the sound and smell of Brandi cooking breakfast. This morning it was coffee, toast, and grits. There was no butter, but Brandi put cinnamon on the toast and it filled the kitchen with a sweet smelling savor. Charles went straight to the table and this morning it seemed he marveled at the little girl who was so smart and so caring. When he looked at her and thought of himself, with tears in his eyes, he asked her, "Why are you so good to me?" Brandi responded, "What do you mean?" He said, "You know I'm a drunk; everybody laughs at us; you don't have a life here; why don't you just leave?"

Brandi did not understand why her dad was saying these things. She finally answered, "Daddy, you are my father, and I love you. Just before mama died, she told me that things might be rough for a while, but she wanted me to take care of you. She said if I was a good girl and took care of you, you would take care of me. That's what we are doing, aren't we? I'm OK, daddy; I just want to take care of you just as I promised mama I would. Don't worry daddy; I'm going to take care of you." With those words, Charles could hardly see through his tears. With those words, he hit rock bottom and apparently that is where God wanted him to be that morning for when his little girl left for school, he began to seek God in earnest. He asked God to deliver him from his broken heart and alcoholism. He asked God to show him how to get back on track so that he could do for his daughter what she had done for him over the years now.

Later that day, Charles got up and cleaned himself up. He went out and began looking for a regular job. He went day after day to place after place until finally he got a decent job that paid good wages. When Sunday came around, he took his daughter to church, and they attended church for the rest of their lives together. In time, Charles changed. He was delivered from his problems and began to live a productive life. Their house became a home again. However, they still had problems. Everyone has problems, but they did just fine. In fact, Charles became a deacon in the church that he later joined. He sent his daughter to college and she graduated. Brandi became a nurse, got married and insisted that her dad live with her family. He became the best granddad in all the community not only to his grandchildren, but to all the children in the neighborhood and church.

What was it that ignited a fire in Charles that set his life on course for rebound and success? It was three words coming from the pure heart of his daughter, "I Love You." Brandi said it; Charles received it, and what a difference it made. It goes to show that having someone to love and demonstrating that love with all your heart can bless people. When you give your best to others, God will send someone to give their best to you. Loving someone will bless your life.

The third essential to happiness is having "something to hope for." The Hebrew word for hope is "yachal;" by implication, to be patient, hope, no matter how painful; stay, tarry, trust, wait. The Greek word for hope is "elpis" which means to anticipate, usually with pleasure; it is expectation or confidence as well as faith and hope. Simply put, when all else is gone and you feel that life makes no sense or has dealt with you unkindly, hope is essential.

African-American Preachers have a way of encouraging each other in the pulpit; while one is preaching, others present will tell him, "Hold your hope, preacher." What they are saying to them is to do your best, stand tall, wait on the Lord, and have faith you are going to make it. Hope then is external and internal encouragement and confidence that what you are expecting will come. This idea is expressed throughout the Bible. Let me give you two scriptures that serve as examples: "Behold, the eye of the LORD is upon them that fear him, upon them that hope in his mercy."(Psalms 33:18) Paul said to the church at Thessalonia: "For what is our hope, or joy, or crown of rejoicing? Are not even ye in the presence of our Lord Jesus Christ at his coming? For ye are our glory and joy." (I Thessalonians 2:19-20)

Believe me when I tell you that in life you must have hope. Hope will see you through dark days, tough times, and ultimately lead you to success from the midst of failure, from defeat to victory.

It is said that decades ago, a Philanthropist and caring man named Eugene Land visited an elementary school in East Harlem. He was there as a guest speaker to talk to the children about business, investments, and how to achieve. Upon his arrival, he noticed that many of the sixth graders looked undernourished. Obviously, they were poor. Some wore ragged, tattered, unclean clothes. Generally, the children looked poorly groomed and he knew that what he had prepared to say to them would not reach them. So, on the spur of the moment, he changed his whole approach and began to talk to them about the struggles of life and what he imagined some of them had experienced. He finished his talk by offering them a challenge. He made them a promise that for all of the children who stayed in school and made decent grades, he would do all within his power to help send them to college. It is said that of those students that he talked to that day, 90 percent of them stayed on task and with his help they, indeed, went to college. This percentage would be unreal at any grade school, much less at a school of underprivileged children. Mr. Land gave those children something that they did not have. Mr. Land gave those children hope. They knew their plight, but they knew there was a better life. These children were smarter than we could imagine. They were presented with a once in a lifetime situation and they took advantage of it. They were given hope and acted upon it.

Consider the story of the horse thief. During the time of antiquity when there were kings in the land, a man approached a kingdom and was caught in the act of stealing a horse. The problem was he was stealing this horse from a king's stable. When he was brought before the king who was told what had happened, the king immediately said, "Take him to the city court and off with his head." Now, before the king and all of his family and court this thief began to beg for his life. "Oh King, have mercy on me, I would never take from such an honorable king. Spare my life and I will teach all your horses to fly." Well, when he king and all his court heard this, they began to laugh uncontrollably. They had never heard such a ridiculous thing. However, it was funny. It made them laugh. For a while it brought great joy to the king who thought to himself, "I will spare his life and he could humor me again some day." So the king told his guards to lock him up for a year and if he did not make the horses fly, he must be put to death.

As the king's men led the horse thief to the prison yard, they began to laugh at him and say, "Old man, you have only delayed the obvious; you will surely lose you life in a year because we all know that horses don't fly." The thief replied, "That's all right; at least I have a year to think of something else; besides in a year's time horses might fly. Or in a year's time, the king might die." The thief was wrong and had no right to attempt to take another man's property. Yet, in his most desperate situation, he did what most people fail to do. The horse thief gave himself some hope. He thought of a better day and believed that somehow, some way, things would change for him, and that change would be for the better. He gave himself some hope. The Bible said that David, in his time of distress, encouraged himself in the Lord. (I Samuel 30:6)

Mr. Addison's simple train of thought has changed my life forever. I have kept these three simple thoughts in mind and have practiced them daily. If I feel a sense of dullness or emptiness in my life, I ask myself these three questions. What am I doing? Do I have someone to love? What is my hope? I know a statement of exclamation belongs behind each question. If there is not one for each question, I begin again to seek to answer those questions in my life. I declare unto you every time I do this I find an internal happiness that compares to nothing I can find in this world.

Step IX:
Three Things That Bring Trouble Into Our Lives

First, let me give credit where credit it due. It was in June of 2004 that I attended the National Baptist Congress of Christian Education. The conference was held in Memphis, Tennessee. I always enjoy attending the National Conventions and I am honored at the privilege of being on the faculty of the National Baptist Congress of Christian Education, NBC, Inc. at this time. That year, as always, I enjoyed attending what we call the Late Night Services. It was while attending one of these services that I heard one of the most profound messages of my life.

It was a sermon preached by one of God's best and unique preachers, Dr. A. Lewis Patterson of Mt. Corinth Baptist Church of Houston, Texas. I have heard Dr. Patterson on several occasions as he is a favorite of all clergy attending the conventions. Believe me, when A. Lewis Patterson is scheduled to preach, it is preachers who fill up the convention halls and auditoriums. He is a preacher's preacher. He is gifted by God, but, moreover, he also takes the time and makes the sacrifice to always give an exegesis of the word of God with simplicity and clarity on a level that challenges the mind to want to dig deeper into his train of thought. On this particular night that I heard Dr. Patterson preach, that is exactly what he challenged me to do. It is from his sermon entitled, "The Cause of All Our Problems", that will allow me to illuminate three things that bring trouble into our lives.

I want to make it clear that I cannot do justice to the actual sermon that Dr. Patterson preached. I make my apology in saying that what I say now is only my perception of the great points that he made about the problems of life that we bring upon ourselves. Let me begin by saying that Satan, the enemy of God, the one who Jesus called the thief, comes but to kill, steal and destroy. (John 10:10) His origin is in Heaven. He was an angel of God according to Isaiah:

> "How art thou fallen from heaven, O Lucifer, son of the morning! How art thou cut down to the ground, which didst weaken the nations! For thou hast said in thine heart, I will ascend into heaven, I will exalt my throne above the stars of God: I will sit also upon the mount of the congregation, in the sides of the north: I will ascend above the heights of the clouds; I will be like the most High. Yet thou shalt be brought down to hell, to the sides of the pit." (Isaiah 14:12-15)

Yes, Lucifer, a fallen angel, was kicked out of Heaven, and his fellowship with God was broken. Now that is what he wants to happen to us. He wants to break up our relationship and our fellowship with God and he does this through temptations and suggestions. His desire is to always cause doubt in our mind. We see this happening in the very beginning. Now, the serpent was more subtle than any beast of the field which the LORD God had made. And he said unto the woman, "Yea, hath God said, Ye shall not eat of every tree of the garden?"(Genesis 3:1) You see, Satan began his interaction with man by raising questions. There's an old saying, "Satan wants to make you doubt in the dark what God told you in the light". Man was created innocent and untried. God placed Adam and Eve in a garden that was paradise on earth. Knowledge of good and evil was unknown to them, but they were warned of what they could eat and what they were to stay clear of, but the fruit of the tree which is in the midst of the garden, God hath said, "Ye shall not eat of it, neither shall ye touch it, lest ye die." And the serpent said unto the woman,

> "Ye shall not surely die: For God doth know that in the day ye eat thereof, then your eyes shall be opened, and ye shall be as gods, knowing good and evil. And when the woman saw that the tree was good for food, and that it was pleasant to the eyes, and a tree to be desired to make one wise, she took of the fruit thereof, and did eat, and gave also unto her husband with her; and he did eat. And the eyes of them both were opened, and they knew that they were naked; and they sewed fig leaves together, and made themselves aprons." (Genesis 3:3-7)

So now Adam and Eve had received knowledge that did not come from God. Here is our first look at educated fools because they had acquired a knowledge that was not of God and His knowledge is wisdom. They learned very quickly that curiosity can kill the cat. Now, they truly knew the difference between those trees. One type of tree was for eating, sustaining life. The other was the tree of prohibition that led to the knowledge of good and evil. The end result: they knew they were naked. They immediately sensed a change. Good and evil became internalized. Now, they were subject to conclusions, personal pleasure, avoiding personal pain, and they acquired self-consciousness. They knew something other than God and they knew that it was not right. So now the creature could choose to obey or disobey the Creator. All was very good until the created sought their own pleasure, their own way. In doing so, they acquired a new nature, a sin nature, a sense of self.

We see this nature very clearly in new born babies. They are only concerned about themselves. They cry when they are hungry, wet, or uncomfortable. Babies want all our attention when they are not asleep. Have you ever noticed how a baby, when old enough to realize mama and dada, will stand between them when they are being affectionate? It is because babies want all the affection and attention for themselves. From this comes that sin nature of I, me, my; its selfishness. From this comes pride, the root of the sin nature. It is a new attitude that things must be done my way, not God's way. Iniquity develops through family habits, folkways and folklore. Families, neighborhood, communities, and nations are developed with the self in mind. We sin because we miss the mark. Our lives are not bent toward pleasing God, but rather our lives are bent toward pleasing ourselves.

Have you realized that people in general do what they want to do and are well intended in those endeavors? Most people do what they do because it gives them pleasure; they see it as something good for them, or they see it as harmless. Sometimes this is done with total disregard to the negative effects or harm to others and themselves. With this train of thought, I want to suggest that there are three basic things that bring trouble into our lives.

First, WE EAT TOO MUCH. Satan always tempts us to change God's order and design for what He intended for us. This is true in almost every area of life. Food is a prime example. Notice how we rarely eat food without changing it. That is Satan's sullen, but subtle way of influencing the way we eat. Let me ask this question. Why do we eat? I am suggesting that we eat for pleasure. We eat because it makes us feel good. We eat for pleasure, not for purpose. Food is for fuel for the body, not for pleasure. Take something as simple as an apple. When eaten as God intended, it is an excellent source of food for fuel. It has at least 18 nutrients and only 80 calories. Yet, we do not eat an apple regularly in its natural form. What do we do? We cook it, add sugar and flour to it and make apple pies. We cook most of the nutrients out of the apple and alter the taste to make it sweeter. Now, an apple that had only 80 calories yields way to slices of apple pie that have 460 calories. We do the same thing across the board with almost all our foods. We cook most of the nutrients out of food, sweeten our foods for a more pleasurable taste, and season our food with spices and condiments until we taste more of the seasoning than we do the actual food. The daily calorie intake is literally killing us, all because we choose to eat for pleasure rather than for purpose.

Did you know that one of the new leading causes of death in the 21st Century is obesity? We simply eat too much. In America, the capitalistic society is saturated with chain restaurants geared to make money with little concern about health. Almost all the fast food chains have super sized entrees. Other eateries have "All You Can Eat Buffets". We, then, are determined to get our money's worth so we eat not until we are full, but rather until we are satisfied that we have gotten our monies worth. I must confess that most of my life I abused my body, not with drugs and alcohol, but with food. I think most people do. We do not mean to, but look at how long it has taken me to get this valuable information about food.

Our body is such a dynamic machine and it takes so much abuse. It is only as the body ages that it begins to have problems dealing with all the abuse we put on it. We can slow down the damage as it has been in my case. Now that I have begun to exercise seriously and pay close attention to what I eat, my body has begun a regeneration process. The human body is truly an amazing gift from God, and we owe it to ourselves to watch what and how much we eat. I am learning that the older I get, the less I need to eat. A person who has to spend much of his time dealing with illness, diseases, and weight problems has less time to do God's work and enjoy life as God intended. One of the causes of our problems is We Eat Too Much and we eat the wrong things. Remember this: whatever we put into our bodies, as it is digested, it affects our body and brain. In other words, we become what we put into our bodies.

The second point to be made is: WE WANT TOO MUCH. Here are the verses of scripture that make this point: "And the woman said unto the serpent, We may eat of the fruit of the trees of the garden: But of the fruit of the tree which is in the midst of the garden, God hath said, Ye shall not eat of it, neither shall ye touch it, lest ye die." (Genesis 3:2-3)

Can you imagine that? God had told Adam and Eve that they could eat from the trees in the garden. They could enjoy any fruit imaginable. In essence, they had everything; it was indeed Paradise. They did not have to work for anything … just get up in the morning and go and eat as they pleased. The only thing God asked of them was, for their own sake, not to eat from the fruit of the tree in the midst of the garden. If they did, they would surely die. Yet, of all they had, they decided they wanted the very thing they could not. Such is human nature. I know I have been there many times—having so much more than others, having abundance and yet desiring that which was not mine, and that which I knew I could not handle. It seems that no matter what we have or obtain, we want just a little bit more. It is said that someone once asked John Rockefeller, in the prime of his life and financial power, "How much money, fame, and power is enough?" Rockefeller replied, "Just a little bit more." Human nature seems to say that no matter how much I have, I will not be happy or satisfied until I get, "just a little bit more". If I just had more money, more power, more influence, more time, and more pleasure, that would be enough. Then, I find out when I get there, that is not enough either.

The third and final cause of our problems is: WE WANT TO KNOW TOO MUCH. If you take a real good look at Genesis 3, you will find that they ate from the forbidden tree not because the fruit tasted good (even though it did), but because they desired to be JUST LIKE GOD. And the serpent said unto the woman,

> "Ye shall not surely die: For God doth know that in the day ye eat thereof, then your eyes shall be opened, and ye shall be as gods, knowing good and evil. And when the woman saw that the tree was good for food, and that it was pleasant to the eyes, and a tree to be desired to make one wise, she took of the fruit thereof, and did eat and gave also unto her husband with her; and he did eat."(Genesis 3:4-6)

I cannot help but wonder how long Adam and Eve had been on the earth before they made this terrible mistake that brought sin into the world? I know they had walked the earth long enough for God to have given them the basic instructions of what to do and what not to do. I know they had been on earth long enough for Adam to have lost some interest in Eve. After all, he was away from her long enough for her to be seduced by the serpent. I wonder did they know just how good they had it in Paradise? Perhaps they had nothing to compare it to so they simply did not know how blessed they were. I do know this one thing: they had been on earth long enough to desire to be as gods. Before they had really come to know themselves and appreciate what they had, they lost it all for the desire to be something God had not called them to be. The same thing that got Satan kicked out of Heaven turned out to be the same thing that got Adam and Eve kicked out of the Garden of Eden: Pride. They were wanting to know and wanting to be like the most high God. Do not misunderstand me; it is one thing to be a humble servant of the God, to submit to our elder brother, Lord and Savior, Jesus Christ, and to aspire to his principles and teachings. This type of man is one who does not want to be like God, to lord over Him or to reign as He reigns; rather, this is a man who seeks the Lord and depends upon Him for his very existence.

But here again, human nature is a sinful nature. It is selfish, self-centered, and self-conceited. Human nature has a way of seeing somebody and at that moment think and honestly believe that "I can do that better than you". I never shall forget my first pastorate. I had been at this little church for almost five years. The people had been good to me, and we had done some good in the church and in the community. However, in time, there arose a group of people who did not share my vision for the future of the church. One deacon who had been an ally for years looked at me differently now. At a conference where I wanted to share my plans for the church, this deacon did something that proved my point.

Toward the end of my discourse when I had said enough and he simply couldn't take anymore, he stood up and said: "Reverend, I've been a deacon for over 35 years and I know more about being a preacher than you do. What you are suggesting we do is ridiculous and we shall not pursue this any further". Now this man was sincere. He was a good man and he meant well, but he was wrong. First of all, how could he know more about being a preacher or Pastor if he had never, in fact, been one? Second, other than 35 years on the Deacon's Ministry, what preacher credentials did he have? Had he been to seminary or to a Bible College? Third, where was his scriptural base for disagreeing with that which I had prayed, fasted, and meditated on for days? The sad part is enough people at the meeting agreed with him and overturned my vision from God to move the church forward.

My point is our human nature tells us we know as much about any subject as the next man even if we have not studied the subject. Think about it. In whose hands would you put your life? The answer: not many people because we tend to think that we know what is best for us in all situations, and we tend to trust our instincts, rather than pursue real answers to questions or seek solutions to real problems. The sad and terrible resolve is that we think that way when it comes to our relationship with God, too. Will you be honest with yourself and say, yes? Too many times I have, according to my knowledge and interpretation of His Word, second guessed God.

Behind all of this, my friend, is Satan. Satan watched in Heaven and wanted from God that which he could not have. He wanted to be responsible to no one, to be restricted by nothing, and to be sovereign. And unfortunately, this is the nature that we have inherited from him.

Yes, it is Satan who keeps the conflicts mentioned in our lives. Satan is deceptive. What if he had told the truth when he engaged in conversation with Eve? What if he had told Eve that he had messed up in heaven and that he had fought against God and lost? In all his talk, he did not mention to her that he had sealed his fate and was eternally damned.

What is our resolve for the cause of all our problems? As always, we look to the scriptures to find the answers. First of all, we must be careful that we do not embrace the things of this world. John, the beloved of Jesus, said it this way:

> "Love not the world, neither the things that are in the world. If any man love the world, the love of the Father is not in him. For all that is in the world, the lust of the flesh, and the lust of the eyes, and the pride of life, is not of the Father, but is of the world. And the world passeth away, and the lust thereof: but he that doeth the will of God abideth forever."(I John 2: 15-17)

Matthew Henry's Commentary explains this verse with simplicity and clarity:

> "The things of the world may be desired and possessed for the uses and purposes which God intended, and they are to be used by his grace, and to his glory; but believers must not seek or value them for those purposes to which sin abuses them. The world draws the heart from God, and the more the love of the world prevails, the more the love of God decays. The things of the world are classed according to the three ruling inclinations of depraved nature. 1. The lust of the flesh, of the body: wrong desires of the heart, the appetite of indulging all things that excite and inflame sensual pleasures. 2. The lust of the eyes: the eyes are delighted with riches and rich possessions; this is the lust of covetousness. 3. The pride of life: a vain man craves the grandeur and pomp of a vain-glorious life; this includes thirst after honor and applause. The things of the world quickly fade and die away; desire itself will ere long fail and cease, but holy affection is not like the lust that passes away. The love of God shall never fail."

The obvious question now is how do we refrain from embracing the world in ways that displease God and are harmful to us? For this resolve, Jesus is our best example:

> "Then was Jesus led up of the Spirit into the wilderness to be tempted of the devil. And when he had fasted forty days and forty nights, he was afterward

an hungred. And when the tempter came to him, he said, If thou be the Son of God, command that these stones be made bread. But he answered and said, It is written, Man shall not live by bread alone, but by every word that proceedeth out of the mouth of God. Then the devil taketh him up into the holy city, and setteth him on a pinnacle of the temple, And saith unto him, If thou be the Son of God, cast thyself down: for it is written, He shall give his angels charge concerning thee: and in their hands they shall bear thee up, lest at any time thou dash thy foot against a stone. Jesus said unto him, It is written again, Thou shalt not tempt the Lord thy God. Again, the devil taketh him up into an exceeding high mountain, and sheweth him all the kingdoms of the world, and the glory of them; And saith unto him, All these things will I give thee, if thou wilt fall down and worship me. Then saith Jesus unto him, Get thee hence, Satan: for it is written, Thou shalt worship the Lord thy God, and him only shalt thou serve. Then the devil leaveth him, and, behold, angels came and ministered unto him."(Matthew 4:1-11)

The hymnologist said it this way: "Yield not to temptation for yielding is sin, each victory will help you, some others to win. Fight manfully onward, dark passion subdue; look ever to Jesus; He will carry you through."

Finally, know that life is lived best when it is lived not for the "self". Only when you give do you receive. You are most blessed when you do for others. Jesus said unto his disciples, "If any man will come after me, let him deny himself, and take up his cross, and follow me." (Matthew 16:24).

Step X:
Lifestyle Changes

It was Christmas 2003. I love the song, "It's The Most Wonderful Time of the Year". That is what Christmas is to most of us. I have always looked forward to Christmas. But, over the years, it has become a most stressful time for me. As a father and husband, I want everything to be just right for everyone. I normally survive the holidays just fine, but not this particular year. I had my usual stressful days and I was also still feeling the pain of the loss of my dear grandmama who had passed away in late October of that year.

Then I received a call on January 2, 2004 that my dad had died. My dad lived in Los Angeles, California. As I have said before, we were not very close, but we kept in touch with each other. My dad, Robert Perkins, was a laid back kind of guy. He was good to people and friendly, but he was a loner. He had been good to me when I asked, but I did not bother him too much. He was 74 years old, but his death came as a shock. Initially, his death did not seem to bother me, but the truth is that the death of my relatives and the usual stress of the Christmas Season took its toll on me.

Like a good soldier, I tried so hard to handle my grief and problems without bothering anyone else. Another factor in this equation was my age. I was 49 years old and I was feeling that, too. I had heard of a mid-life crisis but I have always been confident of myself and had remained focused on those things that were important to me. My God, my family, and my ministry kept me busy and happy. I had no fears and had seemed to be invincible all my adult life until now.

Quite frankly, in the second week of January 2004, I knew I was physically ill and mentally depressed. I had lost two very important people in my life. My doctor diagnosed my illness as gastritis. (There was a war going on in my stomach, and my stomach wasn't winning.) My illness was not life threatening, but the nauseating, painful feeling forced me to deal with my on mortality. I probably preside over 10 to15 funerals each year, and I am always called upon to help families to get through their time of grief and sorrow. I know now that it is ridiculous for anyone to try to handle problems all by themselves. As a Pastor, I preach this all the time: release and express your feelings; encourage one another and encourage yourself. Yet, in one of the darkest times of my life, I did not seek counsel, support, or help from anyone. Part of my unraveling was my pride in not seeking someone to share what I was going through.

I thank God for my wife. It was this patient, sweet, warm, and understanding lady whom I was finally able to open up to and tell just what was going on with me. Then she demonstrated wisdom in telling me that she did not have the answers to my life's riddles; however, she knew I had enough older friends, kin-folk, and comrades to get the special encouragement and answers to what I was going through. So, it was by the grace of God, my wife, doctors, family, and friends that I was able to heal physically and mentally. It took about six weeks, but I was busy, happy, and back to enjoying my life again. What was it that I did that got me back on course and even made life seem steadier that ever?

More than anything else, I came to realize that at my age, I had to make some lifestyle changes if I was going to live a less stressful life as well as keep my energy level up to where I could do all that I wanted to do. What I had to my advantage already was the fact that I have always exercised moderately all my adult life. Even though I was overweight, I was not obese. With a little dedication, I knew I could lose weight. Believe me when I tell you that weight and stress is a death trap waiting to take your life from you. We must do something about the stress, and we must do something about the weight. The good part is that you can see results and feel better in only a few days after you start working on your body by way of diet and exercise.

My sickness was a stomach ailment. I had previously suffered from what is called "acid reflux". Later "gastritis" was diagnosed. Both these ailments are chronic diseases due to bad eating habits and eating at the wrong time. I have found out that both can be controlled and one can be healed if the patient is will-ing to change his diet and exercise regularly. At this point in my life, it was time for me to change my diet anyway. You cannot eat fried, fatty foods or sweets and drink sodas if you want to be healthy and feel good all the time. This is especially true as you get older. I have decided that I do not want to live the afternoon and evening part of my life feeling bad and in bad health. In the book entitled, Fit For Life by Harvey and Marilyn Diamond, they make a unique statement: "If you want to eat more, eat less." That is to say, "the less you eat, the longer you live." This book was published in 1985 and I strongly recommend it for your library.

Here are my suggestions to you about a total lifestyle change. This has worked for me, but it does not necessarily mean it will work for you. Use what you can and then leave the rest; however, do something. I think it is also important to remind you to please see your doctor and get his approval for any form of exercise that you begin.

The first thing that must be understood is that if you are to make a lifestyle change for your good health and strength, it must be with God's help. Daily we must acknowledge Him and ask Him to give us the strength and the will to do what needs to be done. Everyday I wake up with this scripture on my mind: "This is the day which the LORD hath made; we will rejoice and be glad in it." (Psalms 118:24) Now, notice I am using the term "Life Style Change" and not diet. Dieting, in my opinion, is not the answer to a healthy life because as soon as the diet is over, we go right back to doing all of our old bad eating habits.

"Life Style Change" is our recognizing that because our body is changing, we need to modify our life habits to accommodate our changes. Most people simply let nature take its course which means we get weak and therefore we put on weight because we are not as active. We become couch potatoes, and we enjoy eating more as a social outlet as opposed to eating for energy. Then, unfortunately, ailments, sickness, and diseases creep into our lives. Then, with little energy, we have to fight with all our might just to live. Oftentimes, it is a life of physical and mental anguish and pain. I do not know about you, but I do not like pain and suffering. We know we are going to have some of it, but if and when I can avoid it, I do. As has already been stated, it was only after an illness that I decided to take a look at my overall health and I was determined to do something about it. I may get sick and have some prolonged illness and die within a few years, but it will not be because I have overlooked my spiritual and physical fitness. So here is how I went from a sluggish 225 pounds to 193 pounds full of energy.

1. WATER

Your body should have 64 ounces of water everyday for the rest of your life. No excuses; no exception. Hospitals, drugstores, and convenience store sell these 64 ounce bottles. Have you really given thought to water and how it affects everything in this world? Looking at water, you might think that it is the simplest, unimportant thing around. Pure water is colorless, odorless, and tasteless. But it is more that just simple and plain. It is vital for all life on Earth. Where there is water, there is life, and where water is scarce, life is a struggle. Water is called the "universal solvent" because it dissolves more substances than any other liquid. This means that wherever water goes, either through the ground or through our bodies, it takes along valuable chemicals, minerals, and nutrients. And it naturally rids the body of harmful, useless things.

I have always heard that we should drink plenty of water. However, it was not until a friend of mine sent me a 64 ounce jug and told me to drink that amount everyday that I thought I would give water a try. Amazingly, I am hooked on water now. Like most people, I would almost always substitute tea, sodas, juices, etc. for water but now that operation has been reversed. I can go all day and not drink a beverage. I may have half a glass of iced tea with my dinner, but I practice drinking a glass of water before every meal. It helps to fill me up and I have less desire for other beverages which are sometimes full of sugars, preservatives and other things that are not productive for my body. So, what is it about water that makes it so important to us? I am certainly no expert but just think about water as it relates to life. First of all, we develop in our mother's womb in water. Our bodies are comprised of about 85% water. The earth is 1/3 land, 2/3 water. We clean almost everything including our bodies with water. We swim in water for fun and therapy. Water is the base of all that we do. It is a wonder that we do not consume as much water as possible to sustain our bodies. Someone has said that what oil is to a car motor, water is to the body. What electricity is to the light bulb, water is to the body. What blood is to the heart, water is to the blood and to the body. Of all I say about lifestyle changes, I firmly believe that the consumption of an appropriate amount of water daily is the best. Water is a key to physical life and you should drink plenty of it.

2. DIET

I have always been concerned about my health and have always had some kind of work-out regime. However, for years, I forsook my knowledge of having good eating habits. As you all know by now, my lifestyle change was reinforced by recent health problems. I had gone almost 30 years with nothing more than occasional headaches and common flu and cold coughs. There are no guarantees, but I would like to keep my illnesses at that level forever.

I began to change my diet based on my acid reflux problem. I stopped eating peppermint, pepper (I had already decided to stop sprinkling salt on my food in 1998), onion, spices, caffeine, tomatoes, and tomato based products. Further, I learned not to eat heavy foods late a night. I learned to eat smaller portions and to stay away from those things that I know I should not eat. While eating, keep in mind the hand and palm portion; that is to say, eat open hand portions of vegetable, legumes, etc. and palm portions of meat and bread. Eat slowly and enjoy every bite. You will be surprised how full you get when you learn to eat slower. Remember to drink that glass of water before your meal.

I went online and started (as I continue to do to this day) reading and getting various tips about how to eat healthy and have found that www.ediet.com is an excellent website. Some information gained is that ground turkey is so much leaner, better and healthier for you than ground beef. Therefore, we make chili and sometimes hamburgers from ground turkey. Actually, we cannot taste the difference. Put turkey hot dogs in the oven and bake them. I promise you will think you are eating a big thick beef hot dog. It is amazing how turkey is so much better for you. Now, that is not to say that I never have a beef hot dog or beef burger or any of the other things that I mentioned above, but I know they are not as good for me. However, those things are now the exception and not the rule. I have cut back tremendously because I have found other things that I love to eat that are so much more healthy for me. Here are some of the things I have learned to eat that really work for me. When I say work for me, I mean these things help keep the weight off and give me plenty of energy.

For breakfast, I enjoy raisin brand or oatmeal and fruit. In the beginning, I did not like raisin brand cereal. I always thought cereal was for children, but now, I look forward to my breakfast. In fact, when I, on occasion, eat a regular breakfast of eggs, sausage or ham, grits, toast or biscuits, I honestly feel bloated and too full. I become miserable. So, when I eat a breakfast like that (which is rare now), I eat very small amounts. Why raisin brand cereal or oatmeal and fruit? Cereal gives you the rich fiber that you body needs to sustain you and turn food into energy. Oatmeal is great for the heart and lowers bad cholesterol. The fruit is a natural cleansing agent and keeps things moving through your body. Fruit also gives you water base nutrients and that is very important. These foods are great for you. You simply have to adjust to eating them.

NATURAL VITAMINS AND NURTIENT RESOURCES

Nothing takes the place of natural fruits and vegetables for vitamins and nutrients. Sometimes because of what we eat and how we prepare our foods, we lose most of what is good for our body. Therefore, look for some kind of natural supplements to help you along the way. Now, I do not take vitamins but I am a firm believer in the product called "Juice Plus." It is a supplement for fruits and vegetables. The Juice Plus philosophy is to focus on food choices rather than counting calories. It is interesting to note that the average person in China consumes 30% more calories and a pound more of food every day than the average American; yet, most Chinese people do not have a weight problem. It is because of the types of foods they eat. We should eat more nutrient-dense foods. This means consuming a diet rich in fresh raw fruits, vegetables, grains, legumes, nuts and seeds. In fact, the majority of the diet should consist of plant-based food.

Juice Plus guarantees me that daily amount of fruit and vegetables that I need to keep my body strong and energetic. In the beginning, you are supposed to take two capsules of the fruit in the morning and two capsules of the vegetables in the evening. I am down to one of each a day. Why? I have learned to eat plenty of natural fruits and vegetables and it certainly helps me to keep down the cost. You can learn more about Juice Plus online; however, it might not be for everybody, but it sure has been great for me. Another recent product that I have had great results with is Noni Juice. It is a natural juice that is like a tonic for me. It helps to rid the body of toxins, replenishes the natural nutrients and vitamins, and gives you energy. The point that I am making is that you should take the time to find a natural product that is affordable and one that aids in keeping the body healthy and strong. Let your vitamins and nutrients come from natural resources, not ones that are chemically manufactured. The Noni Juice Product also has a website. Get online and find the product that will be a natural aid for your body.

LIVE ACIDOPHILUS & BIFIDUS

Live Acidophilus and Bifidus are types of good bacteria for the body especially if you, like me, have had stomach problems. Your digestive tract is host to about 400 different kinds of bacteria and yeasts. Among these, *Lactobacillus acidophilus* and other members of the *Lactobacillus* family are especially important to your health. Acidophilus is considered "probiotic" bacteria because it helps to maintain intestinal health, and serves as a natural antibiotic against potentially harmful organisms. Taking acidophilus as a nutritional supplement will help maintain the normal balance of beneficial bacteria throughout the body. You can find Acidophilus in some yogurt. Always read the labels to make sure live acidophilus is present. I try to eat at least one cup a day. It is also found in Nu/Tri 1% milk, and yes it is also in Juice Plus.

My breakfast consists of high fiber cereal, Nu/Tri 1% milk and all the fruit I want. I like bananas, strawberries, and pears. It is terrible to say, but as good as fruit is, I had rarely eaten it before now. I have reversed this trend and eat plenty fruit now. I can certainly tell the difference. Be sure to eat breakfast everyday as it is the most important meal because it gets the body awake and working. Skip lunch or dinner, but never skip breakfast. A healthy breakfast will set the stage for your appetite and eating for the rest of the day. I honestly believe that what I eat in the morning curves my desire to eat the rest of the day. Soy milk in your cereal is an excellent substitute for cow's milk. For people like me and many African-

Americans, cow's milk just does not agree with us. Soy milk takes some getting used to. I buy Vanilla soy milk because it has added flavor and decreases flatus (stomach gas). Too much milk and milk products may not be good for you. I love cheese but I have learned that organic cheese does not clog the arteries like regular cheese. Organic cheese is more expensive but the benefits outweigh the cost.

As for snacks, I changed my diet slightly. I have acquired a taste for Granola Bars. They are so good for you but that does not mean you have to stop eating chips, popcorn, etc., however, I suggest eating more granola bars than the other things. Raisins and nuts are also a tasty treat and great for you. Carrots are an excellent crunch snack. I had to acquire a taste for them, but now I eat them like I would eat a bag of chips and they are great for the body. A low fat ice cream with 2% milk poured over it makes a great milkshake. Try it; you will love it. Again, moderation must be the rule for those things that you simply do not want to give up. I choose to break from my regular eating habit only when I have to. I enjoy fast food places only when I travel and have realized that if it is only now and then, I am safe. After the breakfast and snack periods, I eat normal meals. Remember to stay loaded up on vegetables. My doctor told me that most white foods are fatty kinds of foods. Things like potatoes, rice, etc. are good foods, but we should not overdo them. I have learned to eat more baked potatoes as opposed to French fries. Remember, never load your baked potato with butter, sour cream, etc. In other words, learn to be sensible. A good rule that I have developed and it works well for me is to eat my main meal early in the day and to use those hand and fist portions. We simply must learn to cut back on what we eat. I found that I am ok to eat anything I desire if I eat it in small portions (even those things that I know are not in my best interest). Sometimes, the idea is to just satisfy the taste for what you want at a particular time. Learn to eat slowly. When you eat slowly, you do not eat as much.

FISH

By now, you probably know that the most difficult of all foods to digest is meat. As you get older, your body does not have the same vigor to do what it once did. Learning to eat meat in fist portions is a great help to your body. What if you determined to eat meat only once or twice a day? Can you imagine what that would do for you digestive tract and for weight loss?

Now, what about the kind of meat to eat? As I have mentioned earlier, eating large portions of meat won't be doing your body favors as you get older. Do not misunderstand me. There is nothing wrong with beef from time to time, but as you get older, you should consider eating less and less of it. Chicken and pork are white meats and they are much better. However, did you know that chicken today is so processed and so full of steroids for mass production that it does not contain nearly the amount of protein it could? Pork is all right, but keep in mind what pigs eat. Then notice the size of pigs and cows. If the statement, "You are what you eat," has any merit, then these types of meats will indeed cause us to be big. I believe it is true. We are what we eat. It is said that the average man has pounds upon pounds upon pounds of red meat in his bile by the time of his demise. Red meat simply does not digest and leave the body as other meats. That is a lot of unnecessary weigh.

The ideal meat for me is fish. Fish is high in protein and other rich nutrients for the body. It is a lean meat and therefore its lack of fat will reduce the fat produced in your body. I love catfish, red snapper, tuna and salmon. I love fried salmon patties, but I have also acquired a taste for grilled or smoked salmon. A couple of times a week I will eat a tuna sandwich from Subway. Like chicken, there are a lot of ways you can prepare and enjoy fish. The body needs some fat, but do not be fooled. Fat is a killer and we must get rid of it.

If you disagree with anything I tell you, please remember this: you must do something to drop your weight. Too much weight brings on all kinds of health problems. That is a fact. I dropped my weight from 225 lbs to 193 lbs and I am so happy about that. I am solid and have maintained this weight (give or take a few pounds) for years. However, according to my BMI (body mass index), I am still overweight. I am not obese, but I am overweight for my body size and age. The weight that I should be in order to be at my healthiest is 184 or below. I hope to reach that weight one day.

3. EXERCISE

I have always been very athletic and have worked out at the gym or YMCA. Perhaps that is one of the reasons I have had fairly good health and strength. However, I have never been on any kind of plan to reduce weight or to build muscles. My exercising has always been, in a sense, an outlet or to have fun. And even now I try to keep it like that. However, know that even the Bible commands us to be concerned about our body: "I beseech you therefore, brethren, by the mercies of God, that ye present your bodies a living sacrifice, holy, acceptable unto God, which is your reasonable service." (Romans 12:1) That certainly says to me that I ought to do all I can to preserve this body to present to God daily for his service. I have a responsibility to God to take care of my body so that He can use it. How can I serve God if I am tired all the time, sick all the time, have no energy, or not feeling good about my appearance. My body belongs to Him.

In Paul's letter to the Church of Corinth he states: "What? Know ye not that your body is the temple of the Holy Ghost which is in you, which ye have of God, and ye are not your own? For ye are bought with a price: therefore glorify God in your body, and in your spirit, which are God's." (I Corinthians 6:19-20)

Yes, it is clear that we must take care of our body, and that is done primarily by the manifestation of the Holy Spirit working in us. Exercising is not the main thing in taking care of the body. I suggest fasting and praying, and watching what we put into our temple. We must abstain from smoking. If you choose to drink alcohol, be moderate in your drinking.

Paul advises Timothy: "For bodily exercise profiteth little: but godliness is profitable unto all things, having promise of the life that now is, and of that which is to come." (I Timothy 4:8) Doctors have studied and determined that nothing will take off weight and give you energy like eating properly and exercising. There is no other way. Pills or diet will not suffice. It will take a lifestyle change and that means that you must be willing to eat properly and exercise from now on until the day you go to be with the Lord. The one thing I have discovered that should be great news for you is that it really does not take a lot of exercise. The exercise simply must be consistent and persistent. That means for whatever form of exercise you decide to do, you must do it almost daily and for at least a 30 minute period of time. For me that is not hard. As a matter of fact, I have come to look forward to doing my exercises almost every day. I say almost every-day because it is important to rest your body too. My regime is to exercise at least 5 days a week and to rest my body two days a week.

My exercise routine is never more than 30 minutes a day, and I do different things each day. I will do a stationary bicycle ride one day. I may lift weights (not for bulking but for toning my muscles) another day, or I will work out on a cross training machine. Then, perhaps, I may walk or jog. I never do more than 30 minutes because that has been proven to be enough. Now, when I finish exercising (if at the YMCA), I will go into the steam room or whirlpool and have some relaxing water therapy. Believe me, I feel so much better and it does not take all day. Also, it is something I know I can do the rest of my life. That is why I call it lifestyle change. Make it fun, make it easy and you will succeed. Be patient and do not try to lose weight over a week or month. It took me over a year to lose my weigh, but I did it.

To sum this all up, don't be afraid to reinvent yourself. Most people can lose weight, feel better and have good health and lots of energy, but it requires our willingness to make some changes. You should be tired of doing the same old things all the time. Change your train of thought. You can become a brand new person that you and others will be excited about it. It might be difficult at first, but let that be the fun of it. Laugh at it and press on through until you see some real changes in your attitude, body, and your entire life. The bottom line is that we simply eat too much. We live to eat, but we ought to eat to live. If you want to live longer, eat less. Also, learn to eat more of the things that your body was truly designed for you to eat. Raw fruits, vegetables and plenty of lean mean will bless your body. Then know that when you start eating differently, your body may take you through some painful experiences for a few days. Your body is simply cleansing itself of all the toxins and poisons that have settled in your body. Keep eating good things and you will feel better not to mention how you energy level will rise.

Do yourself a favor. Have regular check-ups with your doctor. He can help you to know your capabilities and limitations. I see my doctor every six months for a general check up. That is how serious I am about guarding my health. Remember, "An ounce of prevention is worth a pound of cure."

Step XI:
Dare To Be Different; Dare To Be You

Have you ever thought about how unique and distinct nature and human beings are? It is said that no two snowflakes have the same prints. Six billion plus people are presently on the face of this earth and all of us have different fingerprints. Of all the computers ever made and upgraded, the greatest and most dynamic is the human body. God is so particular and meticulous about us until the Bible says that even the hairs on our head are numbered. (Matthew 10:30)

The Psalmist says it like this:

> "I will praise thee; for I am fearfully and wonderfully made: marvellous are thy works; and that my soul knoweth right well. My substance was not hid from thee, when I was made in secret, and curiously wrought in the lowest parts of the earth. Thine eyes did see my substance, yet being unperfect; and in thy book all my members were written, which in continuance were fashioned, when as yet there was none of them. How precious also are thy thoughts unto me, O God! how great is the sum of them! If I should count them, they are more in number than the sand: when I awake, I am still with thee." (Psalms 139:14-18)

Everything that God did in Creation He did with our best interest in mind and heart. The earth is so positioned that where it rests in space and turns on its axis the sun provides enough heat and light to sustain us. If the earth were farther away or closer to the sun, the earth would either burn up or freeze. Either one of those conditions would mean our doom. The earth is so tilted on an axis that we have seasons: summer, fall, winter, and spring. The world turns so as to give us day and night every 24 hours. Rain, sleet, snow, clouds, sunshine and night time give us a variety so that each day has its own unique presentation.

If I have learned anything about life, it is this: I am a creation of God. No one was created for the purpose for which I was. I can do something like no one else can do. I have but this one life. I must find and fulfill my destiny.

This, then, is the adventure of life: to seek or come to know your destiny and fulfill it. Only through Christ our Lord can we do this and in the process comes abundant and everlasting life. That is the promise of God. If only people could come to this realization. I embrace these words that I read somewhere and now have framed in my mind: "Who you are is God's gift to you; what you do with your life is your gift to God." Thus it becomes our privilege and honor to be a gift to God. Hold fast to those good and positive things refusing those temptations that go against the righteousness of God. Lift high the banner of God, abhorring those things that are not of God. How do we accomplish that? Serve mankind and get busy living by finding and fulfilling destiny. I have discovered that in doing so, you will, in some way, be helping others. Again I say, have something to offer the world that only you can offer. You must learn to see yourself as one who can make a difference in the world around you. Take small steps; start in your home and then proceed at school or work. Next, work in your church and community, and watch as you take off to who knows where in making a difference in this world.

I recently watched the movie "Aviator" which is about the life and times of Howard Hughes. Before watching the movie, all I knew about him was that he was, at one time, considered to be one of the richest men in the world. I thought that was something, but the truth is his riches were more than his money or what money could buy. Since watching the movie, I have been reading books and watching documentaries about Howard Hughes's life.

I have concluded that what really made him rich was not his money or what it could buy, but rather his love for aviation and his pursuit of it. Because of this, we all are so much better off when it comes to flying both militarily and commercially. Read about him and you will discover that he is indeed an aviation hero, not to mention what his pursuits did to advance technology. Yet, his life was filled with tragedy because of a then unknown mental disorder—Obsessive Compulsive Disorder. If only he could have known about his illness and dealt with it the same way he pursued his love of planes, he might have been a happier man.

But despite his illness, compulsiveness, and a baggage of promiscuous living, he was a great man in that he gave so much to society. I have come to admire him in spite of his illness and faults because he did not stray from his passion. In my thinking, he did not forsake his gift and calling from God: advancing the world in aviation. Observing Howard Hughes's life, this notion in my mind is reenforced: it is not what money can buy that makes you rich, but rather it's what money cannot buy that makes you rich.

The more I learn and know about life the more I realize just how little I know. Let me continue to share with you some of the things I have learned that you must work on in order to know who you are. You really do not have to dare to be different because you already are different. You are who God made you to be, but you must do a great work on yourself. Paul explained it this way to his spiritual son, Timothy: "Study to shew thyself approved a workman that needeth not to be ashamed, rightly dividing the word of truth." (2 Timothy 2:15)

This idea is to me the great challenge of our lives. The ultimate end allows us to be a tremendous help and encouragement to others. But the process of this task allows us to learn and to know who we really are. At the time that Paul writes these words, he is facing an uncertain future. Yet, he is so confident in the outcome of his future that he is encouraging and giving others sound advice. Paul tells Timothy that the Christian life is not easy and that he could not be strong in himself, but rather he must be strong in the grace that is in Christ Jesus. Then, he makes another key point in telling him that whatever you learn from me and other mature Christians, be sure to pass it on to others. In other words, be sure to be a mentor to someone else. There is nothing more gratifying than helping someone to grow and to be the best self they can be. But you cannot take people where you have not been. In this verse, then, Paul makes three basic points about "the self."

First, you must be a diligent self. Studying self has nothing to do with books and teaching others until you become diligent. Study means to be earnest, prompt, and giving yourself painstakingly to a purpose or cause. In this case, the studying is to be applied to yourself. It is an inward analysis of who you are. It is seeking God so that you might come to know your capabilities and limitations. Then, it is learning how to live within those boundaries. Certainly, as you grow, your boundaries will expand, but it takes time and effort. In other words, there is some pressure in being a diligent self.

I have a song that often comes to mind in my ongoing pursuit of my diligent self: "It's me, it's me, its me, O Lord, standing in the need of prayer." As you mature in this quest, you come to know who you are and whose you are. Believe me, knowing that is empowering. You see the first work is on yourself. God will not bless me, anoint me, or possess me to help others until I have fully surrendered myself to Him.

I heard a preacher say that when you have the word rooted in you, you have authority. When you have the Holy Spirit present in you, you have God's power.

That is empowerment. Therefore, we are not just what our vocation defines us as; instead, we are that plus spiritual authority and power. You do not have to be the CEO on the job or the supervisor, but people will be drawn to you because they recognize your inward authority and power that God has placed in you. Whatever you position, you will make a difference in the lives of others. God will privilege you to impact others in the most dynamic ways, and there is nothing more rewarding than that.

The second point about "the self" is that now you desire to be approved of God, rather than man. Did you know that most people go through life wanting to please man rather than God? As a Pastor, I have had people come to me and give money to the church. They would say, "Now, Pastor, when I die, say some good and pleasant things about me so that the people might think well of me." Can you imagine that? They have no concern about whether God is pleased with their lives or where they might spend eternity; they simply want to be remembered by people as a good person.

You have heard the cliché "Keeping up with the Joneses." Some people allow others to dictate to them how they live their lives. If the Joneses get a new car, then the family next door feels the need to get a new car. If the Joneses go on vacation to Niagara Falls, then the family next door plans a trip to Europe in order to out do the Joneses.

What a sad way to live your life, not to mention that this kind of thinking is only temporal. You deserve more than that. You should want to do things born out of your own desires—things that will benefit you now and later. You want to be a person concerned not only about temporal things, but about things of eternity also. This type of thinking can only be achieved when you live you life for Christ. You want to live in such a way that God approves of you now and forever. Presently, you are living one of two ways: you are either living a life approved by God or a life of which God is ashamed. There is no middle ground and the latter life is simply useless and dangerous.

Dr. Gardner Taylor, one of the great preachers of the 20th Century, tells a story that proves my point. Two angels stood from the balcony of a mansion in heaven and watched while others were entering the pearly gates of Heaven. One day they noticed Jesus had come to the gate to receive two men who were coming home. As they watched the three men walk into the gate, there was a commotion behind them. They looked away momentarily and when they looked on the three men again, one angel asked the other, "Now which one of those men is Jesus." The two men in life had become so close in actions and personality to the Lord (their talk, their walk, their attitude, their love, etc.) until the angels could not tell one from the other. That is how we want to live. We want to live so close to God until when others look upon us, they will see a resemblance of Christ in us. People are not drawn to you, but they are drawn to the Christ in you. You offer others something that they can get nowhere else in this world. That is because who you are is unique and special. Now, that is being empowered.

The third point is the "disciplined self." When you are diligent and approved of God, you learn to be disciplined in your life. In reality, you are becoming a disciple of Christ. Jesus is not just your Savior; He is your Lord also because you are living to do His will. Again, this not only takes time and effort, but it also requires your old self to die and daily you will be challenged to bring forth the best that is in you. It is there in you but you must bring the best self forward.

Listen to the Apostle Paul: "This I say then, Walk in the Spirit, and ye shall not fulfill the lust of the flesh. For the flesh lusteth against the Spirit, and the Spirit against the flesh: and these are contrary the one to the other: so that ye cannot do the things that ye would." (Galatians 5:16-17) Everyday of your life there is a war going on inside of you—the flesh against the spirit; the disciplined self verses the undisciplined self. The way your spirit wins over the flesh is by denying the flesh. "Then said Jesus unto his disciples, If any man will come after me, let him deny himself, and take up his cross, and follow me." (Matthew 16:24)

When you make this your priority, then you win daily. It is not easy; the temptations are real, but as you grow in the faith, you grow in grace and you become the disciple of Christ that He intended for you to be. Think about it. What is a higher vocation in life than being a disciple of Christ? Spirit filled, Spirit led, Spirit controlled—all yield a strong prayer and devotional life that ultimately lead to a life of service. This way of life will leave you blessed and those around you will be blessed as well. I dare you to be different; I dare you to be you.

I do not recall the source for the following statement, but I believe it to be profound in defining who a person really is. So, now I ask you what I believe to be the most profound of all questions for a person to answer. Who am I? Why am I Here? Where am I Going? I believe if a person seeks to answer these questions periodically in life, this person will become a better person even if he can never quite fully answer the questions.

I do know this: whether you realize it or not, we all change every seven to ten years. If you do not believe that, just look at what you were doing seven to ten years ago. Consider where you worked, where you lived, what interested you most, what was most valuable to you, and where you spent most of your time. Study it long enough and you will see that you have changed whether you wanted to or not. Some things you used to do you just cannot do anymore. Some things would just be inappropriate for you to do now that you are older. I am confident that you will be very different ten years from now. At some point in life, we must understand that the only constant in life is God. Everything else must change. We must change to be more like Him (God the Father, through Jesus Christ), or we will grow farther and farther away from Him. Of this I am sure.

So ask yourself, "Who Am I?" I mean when you take off your worldly mask and clothes, where you live, worldly influences, family, friends, and acquaintances, who are you? When you take away those trappings that you have wrapped yourself in and are left to your own nakedness, who are you? As my friend, Rev. Gene Washington, often says, "Who are you way down in the city of your soul?"

The Apostle James describes the self as a *vanishing vapor:*

> "Whereas ye know not what shall be on the morrow. For what is your life? It is even a vapour, that appeareth for a little time, and then vanisheth away. For that ye ought to say, If the Lord will, we shall live, and do this, or that. But now ye rejoice in your boastings: all such rejoicing is evil. Therefore to him that knoweth to do good, and doeth it not, to him it is sin." (James 4:14-17)

That is to say, we have no guarantees about the future for tomorrow may never come. This adage is true: "Yesterday is in the tomb of time. Tomorrow is in the womb of time.

All we have is now. That is why we call it the present." All we seek to do and to be should be in the acknowledgment of God, the Father who made us. Paul clarifies our identity on the earth by saying: "For in him we live, and move, and have our being; as certain also of your own poets have said, For we are also his offspring." (Acts 17:28)

Now it is in the Proverbs of Solomon that we find the personal challenge of discovering who we are in our hearts. Consider Proverbs:

> "When thou sittest to eat with a ruler, consider diligently what is before thee: And put a knife to thy throat, if thou be a man given to appetite. Be not desirous of his dainties: for they are deceitful meat. Labour not to be rich: cease from thine own wisdom. Wilt thou set thine eyes upon that which is not? for riches certainly make themselves wings; they fly away as an eagle toward heaven. Eat thou not the bread of him that hath an evil eye, neither desire thou his dainty meats: For as he thinketh in his heart, so is he: Eat and drink, saith he to thee; but his heart is not with thee." (Proverbs 23:1-7)

Now what Solomon, who is regarded as one of the wisest man ever to live, is saying is: Do not waste your life trying to be rich on this earth for riches will come and riches will go. Strange that Solomon would say that because he was also regarded as one of the wealthiest men to ever live. Maybe that is why Solomon could make such a declarative statement. He justifies his statement again in Ecclesiastes: "Vanity of vanities, saith the Preacher, vanity of vanities; all is vanity." (Ecclesiastes 1:2)

Vanity is in the same family with vapor in that they are both temporal. They are soon to be gone. Jesus said it like this in Matthew: "For what is a man profited, if he shall gain the whole world, and lose his own soul? or what shall a man give in exchange for his soul? For the Son of man shall come in the glory of his Father with his angels; and then he shall reward every man according to his works."(Matthew 16:26-27) He says it again in Mark:

> "For what shall it profit a man, if he shall gain the whole world, and lose his own soul? Or what shall a man give in exchange for his soul? Whosoever therefore shall be ashamed of me and of my words in this adulterous and sinful generation; of him also shall the Son of man be ashamed, when he cometh in the glory of his Father with the holy angels." (Mark 8:36-38)

Now what Solomon implies or infers is that when we crave the things of this world, our thinking makes us dreadful wicked souls. Why? It is because our appetite is for the here and now, rather than what makes us most rich: those things of Heaven. I can pause right here and ask: Who are you?" What do you think about most? Do you think about Heaven more than things of this world or vice versa? Listen to Jesus:

> "But rather seek ye the kingdom of God; and all these things shall be added unto you. Fear not, little flock; for it is your Father's good pleasure to give you the kingdom. Sell that ye have, and give alms; provide yourselves bags which wax not old, a treasure in the heavens that faileth not, where no thief approacheth, neither moth corrupteth. For where your treasure is, there will your heart be also." (Luke 12:31-34)

Am I telling you that we should not want to have earthly things in this life? Am I telling you that we should not pursue our dreams and goals to be somebody and have riches, fortune, or fame? Am I suggesting we cannot have money in the bank and take trips around the world? No, No, No!!! I am not saying that at all. It is one thing to be industrious, but another thing to consume oneself for money. Look at what people will do for money. You remember the O'Jays song:

"For the love of money, people will lie, rob and steal; a woman will sell her precious body for that mean green." Paul says: "For the love of money is the root of all evil which while some coveted after, they have erred from the faith, and pierced themselves through with many sorrows." (1 Timothy 6:10) We must make a living, we must provide for our families, but we are not to love money. Making money and spending money should not be the thing that defines who we are.

I am clearly reenforcing that the way you come to know who you are and to be blessed with abundance is to seek God first. I am saying the things of this world that you think in your heart you want to obtain and do will be meaningless if you do not have God First in your heart.

Let me give you some examples. Look at Dr. Martin Luther King, Jr., the great revolutionist of our times. His influence has changed the world forever; dream or no dream, this man has made an impact like none of his day. He did not live long, but he had a full life. He did things, went places, experienced mountain top highs and valley lows, joys and sorrows, victories and defeat that few men experience. Was he perfect? No, he had faults. Did he let his faults and failures stop him? No, he stayed the course of his calling. Was he rich? No, not materially; he did not leave his children a penny to go to college; nor did he own his own home, but because of who he was, others who had money ensured that his children went to college and that his family had a place to live. Was he famous? Yes, because he had a message from God. The point that I am making is because He put God First and accepted the calling that God put on his life on earth, he gave more than he received; and in heaven he gained more than he lost because the earth and its possessions are temporal, but Heaven is eternal. Remember Job's words: "Naked came I out of my mother's womb, and naked shall I return thither: the LORD gave, and the LORD hath taken away; blessed be the name of the LORD." (Job 1: 21)

Never forget that we are just stewards, that we do not own anything. There have been others who had tremendous callings on their lives like Dr. King, yet they did not fare as well. Look across this country in the fields of religion, business, entertainment, and sports and be reminded of many gifted, talented, famous and rich people. Nevertheless, they could never separate their image from who they really were. With all they had, they never knew their purpose. Their lifestyles of self-indulgence consumed them. Some were strung out on drugs; some lost their way to ungodly, intolerable sexual habits, and some even lost their lives because of their violent speech and lifestyle. Their very gifts and talents, their fame and fortune that could have been a blessing to them and others had become a curse upon their lives. If they could, I am sure, they would give back all the fortune and fame to have the life God intended for them. With God, less can be more.

I agree that there is a fine line between separating the image of someone from the real person and serving others as opposed to being self-serving. The real problem is that most of us do not spend enough time thinking. Remember as a man thinketh in his heart, so is he. When we do think, we often think about the wrong things.

What, then, is our solution? Well, I want to suggest that what really defines you is your relationship with God and people. You see, that is the stuff that remains in your soul. That is the stuff you can carry to heaven with you.

First, you must come clean and stay clean in your relationship with God. In other words, to know who you are, we must get completely naked (be honest) before God. We must confess all our sins before Him and acknowledge Him as Lord and Savior. This idea is what being born again is all about. Life before knowing Christ is just natural, carnal, fleshly, and temporary. This is why Jesus told Nicodemus (a very prominent, decent, good, highly religious man), "Verily, verily, I say unto thee, Except a man be born again, he cannot see the kingdom of God." (John 3:3) But that is not the end of the process but instead is only the beginning. Do you know that the one thing that keeps us from the presence of God is sin? You can never become the complete self, pure in heart, and the whole creature God calls you to be until you are free from sin. Therefore, even after being born again, we must stay before God seeking forgiveness. Remember what Peter asked Jesus: "Then came Peter to him, and said, Lord, how oft shall my brother sin against me, and I forgive him? till seven times? Jesus saith unto him, I say not unto thee, Until seven times: but, Until seventy times seven." (Matthew 18: 21-22)

Never let the enemy (Satan) make you think you are not worthy to go to God in prayer to be forgiven of your sins. In fact, Paul says it like this: "Let us therefore come boldly unto the throne of grace, that we may obtain mercy, and find grace to help in time of need." (Hebrews 4:16)

When is our time of need? All the time. And what is our greatest need? It is a need for God, a need for the Kingdom of God. It is not enough to be baptized if you want to be a disciple, not if you want to know who you are. Daily, sometimes hour by hour, we need to cry out to God. God forgive me and give me self-worth. Let me know my existence: the what, when, where, and how of it. Then and only then can I know my purpose and know how to treat my neighbors. Yes, it is all about relationships. We cannot love others, nor love ourselves until we first love God. Please know that God does love us so very much. No matter what it appears to be, God loves us. He frowns at our wayward ways, but He smiles upon mankind, His crown creation. Remember this statement as a way of knowing how much God loves us: You did not ask to come here, and you surely do not know when and how you are going to leave this earth so our existence between birth and death is totally an act of God—a God who loves us, who cares for us, and who has a plan for us. He asks one thing of us: get to know me so that I can tell you who you are, why you are here, and where you are going.

Consider the story of the master house builder. He labored most all his life working for another man building houses. As gifted as he was at his trade, his problem was that he did his work strictly for the money. He could not see the beauty of his accomplishments. He did not appreciate his calling. After approximately 25 years of service, his employer had a surprise for him. As he was approaching retirement, he told him, "I want you to build me one more house and you can retire. You'll have a decent pension and you can do other things." But the man had come to a point in his life where he did not care for his craft anymore. Clumsily, slothfully, and cutting corners, the man built this last house for his employer. Finally, when the house was built, the man went to his boss and told him the job was completed and asked for him to come and inspect the house. The employer looked at him, tossed him a set of keys and said, "No need for that because the house you just built is yours." At that point, the master builder thought about how he had built the house and walked away in despair. Why? He knew he had not done his best on a project that was now his home.

In many instances, this is how we approach life. We live life just for the money, the fortune, the fame, not realizing that the true blessing in life is not what we do, but how well we do it. If we live our lives to honor God, then the end result will be a well-spent life, abundant and rewarding to the very end and even into eternity.

If anyone should ask you who you are, tell him "I am a child of God". If anyone should ask you why are you here, tell him "I am here to fulfill my destiny". And if anyone should ask you where you are going, tell him "I am going up yonder to be with my Lord".

Bibliography

Addison, Joseph, Cato: "A Tragedy and Selected Essays". Ed. Christine Dunn Henderson & Mark E. Yellin. Indianapolis: Liberty Fund, 2004

All Bible Quotes: King James Version, Life Application Study Bible, 1988, Tundale House Publishers, Inc., Wheaton, Il 60189

Barth, Karl. Portrait of Karl Barth. Contributors: Robert McAfee Brown, Georges Casalis. Publisher: Doubleday. Garden City, New York: 1963

Bonhoeffer, Dietrich. The Cost of Discipleship, Macmillan Publishing Company, 1963, Mass Market Paperback, Biblio.com

Diamond, Harvey and Marilyn. Fit For Life, Warner Books, Inc., New York, New York 10103, Copyright 1985

Matthew Henry's Commentary. SwordSearcher.com 1995-2007 Brandon Staggs. All rights reserved. P.O. Box 140478, Broken Arrow, Ok 74014, USA

Poem: "House by the Side of the Road", Samuel Walter Foss, Public Domain, 1899.

Spurgeon, Charles Haddon. The Treasury of David. Published by Guardian Press, 1976, Vol. 11, pages 384, 385.

What The Bible Says ... To The Minister, "The Minister's Personal Handbook", Second Edition, 1996, by Alpha-Omega Ministries, Inc., Published by Leadership Ministries Worldwide, page 357; 359.

Walvoord, J.F., Zuck, R.B., Dallas Theological Seminary. 1983-c 1985. The Bible Knowledge Commentary: An Exposition of the Scriptures. Victor Books: Wheaton, Il.

978-0-595-47059-
0-595-47059-9

CPSIA information can be obtained
at www.ICGtesting.com
Printed in the USA
LVHW03s0316080918
589515LV00001B/23/P